Freedom
from Toxic
Relationships

Freedom from Toxic Relationships

Moving on from the Family, Work, and Relationship Issues That Bring You Down

Avril Carruthers

TARCHER/PENGUIN

a member of Penguin Group (USA)

NEW YORK

JEREMY P. TARCHER/PENGUIN
Published by the Penguin Group
Penguin Group (USA) LLC
375 Hudson Street
New York, New York 10014

USA · Canada · UK · Ireland · Australia
New Zealand · India · South Africa · China

penguin.com
A Penguin Random House Company

First published in Australia by Allen & Unwin 2011
First Tarcher/Penguin paperback edition 2013
Copyright © 2011 by Avril Carruthers

Most Tarcher/Penguin books are available at special quantity discounts for bulk purchase for sales
promotions, premiums, fund-raising, and educational needs. Special books or book excerpts also can
be created to fit specific needs. For details, write: Special.Markets@us.penguingroup.com.

Library of Congress Cataloging-in-Publication Data

Carruthers, Avril.
Freedom from toxic relationships : moving on from the family, work,
and relationship issues that bring you down / Avril Carruthers.
p.   cm.
Includes index.
ISBN 978-0-399-16611-2
1. Interpersonal relations.   2. Interpersonal conflict.   3. Adult
children—Family relationships.   I. Title.
HM1106.C372   2013   2013028977
302—dc23

Printed in the United States of America
1 3 5 7 9 10 8 6 4 2

Book design by Gretchen Achilles

Contents

Acknowledgments

My husband for constant support, truly excellent coffee, fragrant stirfries, salads and hysterical jokes. My sister for being an intelligent and insightful springboard on which to bounce ideas. My daughter for reading whatever I put in front of her for feedback with only the tiniest of eye rolls, and then coming up with a well-reasoned and constructive assessment. For illuminating comments, stories, valuable feedback and constructive suggestions: Archie, Michelle Barrett, Christine Bennett, Dianne Blayney, Robyn Drummond, Leanda Elliot, Joni Harvey, Wendy Lohse, Dr John Merchant, Sharon Rundle, Euan Schaewel. The team at Allen & Unwin: Maggie Hamilton, Kathy Mossop, Vanessa Pellatt, Susin Chow and fisheye design for astute insight and support. My clients and supervisees—as always, my best teachers.

Contact websites

www.avrilcarruthers.com
www.clairvision.org

Introduction

Transpersonal psychotherapy, the context in which this book is based, often includes meditative states and energy work—the sensing of flows of energy linked to emotional states. Deep spaces of perception and receptivity give access to extraordinary vision. They are not things we normally see with everyday eyes. In fact, in the cold light of commonly agreed-upon reality, some people find it hard to reconcile what they have themselves experienced in spaces of deep awareness. This is particularly the case from the viewpoint of Western science-based education and the dominance of left-brain logic and physical evidence.

For others, the memory of what they have seen and felt in their deeper knowingness convinces them that reality is not always as it appears on the surface. The profound transformations that emerge from these experiences are proof of their value and their meaning. We might hesitate to mention our very personal inner reality, but it doesn't mean it's not real, and many might relate to the stories in this book.

Our own particular inner landscape might be a place of safety and connection or, at times, a dark, lonely abyss in which we feel cut off, abandoned, unseen or unrecognized. The ways in which these inner states work with our consciousness are through dreams, symbols, and images of various structures that owe their particular form to our cultural background or personal experiences. Powerfully meaningful and often profoundly transformative, they show us the way out to health and wholeness. They allow us the means for redemption.

Perhaps you already practice meditation or have felt the flow of energy through your body while practicing qi gong, tai chi or yoga. Perhaps you have felt the effects of an oppressive, controlling or draining relationship on your health or your equilibrium, and wish to understand it and be free of it.

Energetic cords are unconscious—often sentimental or compulsive—emotional ties to past and present relationships, preconditioned by our wounds. They are made of toxic emotions such as fear, guilt, blame, hatred, obligation, grasping need or pain. Learning to be aware of, detach from and transcend this very human trap comprises the main content of this book. Esoteric terms are used where there are no simple equivalents in lay language to provide a frame of reference to describe deeper experiences. These terms refer to the subtle bodies: *astrality* or the *astral body* of our thoughts and emotions; the *etheric* or life-force body; the *Egoic* body, which is our representation of spirit incarnate; and *samskara*—the Sanskrit word for a scar on the astral body. They provide a basis for understanding the sticky, magnetic nature of energetic cords and the difference between a cord relationship and one that is not tied by conditioned emotions, but coexists in Egoic presence. This concept introduces the possibility to connect consciously and at will with those we love in an eternal present that goes beyond geographical space and even beyond death.

The stories of the bewildering, toxic effects of energetic cords derive from the forty-odd years of my experience and practice. Working with the unconscious and higher consciousness—and their wondrous depictions of psychic, emotional and physical states—the transformative insight of conscious perception is a constant revelation, whether they are symbolic representations or more tangible, felt-as-though-real experiences. This modality remains an invaluable tool for interior knowing and a road map for change that inspires a sense of the numinous in its travelers. In this landscape, sacred rituals then follow naturally. Their power helps people heal long-nursed hurts, paralyzing fears, puzzling conditions of ill health, and frozen development that prevents people from leading lives that are free— or even just finding out what they really want.

I have recorded my clients' individual perceptions of cords as faithfully as possible, while changing their names and identifying details. Some stories are combined where similarities indicate common experiences to which many people might relate and to draw together elements of essential truth. I am deeply grateful for the generosity of all who have graciously shared their explorations and perceptions.

AVRIL CARRUTHERS

Part One

What Is a Toxic Relationship?

RELATIONSHIPS form an interweaving fabric in our lives. They connect us and give us meaning. They can be transforming. They can also bring us down. Whenever we have a close or intense relationship with someone, ties form that may be beneficial or harmful. We can mistakenly believe we find our true Selves reflected in another person, only to lose our sense of Self, our identity, because it is not a true reflection. We may no longer know who we are as an individual and, instead, become defined by our relationship or our place in it.

Chapter 1

Where it all begins

Getting engaged or married in medieval times entailed the ritual of handfasting in which the lovers' wrists crossed right to right and left to left in a hand clasp, creating the figure eight symbol of eternity. A rope or ribbon was looped over their thumbs and joined wrists during the ceremony and when the pair gently drew their hands apart, a knot formed in the ribbon. It led to the expressions "tying the knot" or "getting hitched" and signals a commitment to a lifetime of happiness and joy, bringing up a family, mutual support and comfort. In the old tradition, if the couple wished to separate, they simply untied the knot. For most of us, however, when the relationship turns out not to be joyous, severing the ties between us is far more problematic than undoing a knot in a ribbon. These sticky attachments generally begin long before we stand with our lover declaring to keep only to him or her for the rest of our lives. It's shown by other expressions commonly in use.

When we refer to adult children on the brink of independence we often speak of the need to cut the umbilical cord. We also talk about cutting apron strings—usually with mothers or wives. We know that we can internalize our mother's voice and our parents' warnings, values and expectations from when we were small, and how those can weigh us down. We know what someone means when he describes being "under someone's thumb" or having someone "on his back." We hear of people being "joined at the hip" or those who "married his mother/her father." All these phrases describe attachments that people feel are oppressive or just somehow unhealthy. In this book, they are what I refer to as toxic relationships.

All our intense relationships—whether with a boyfriend or girlfriend, a sibling or other relative, even a boss or close friend—have subtle but tangible emotional or energetic attachments that begin to have lives, and influences, of their own. These energetic connections, or cords, can develop over time or form instantly, such as when people fall in love at first sight. They can affect our emotional state, our energy and health, and can even let us know what the other person is doing, regardless of how close or far apart we may be. The reason for this is that these connections are actually conduits conveying energy in the form of emotions and thoughts from one person to the other.

Energetic cords do not depend on proximity and can outlast the actual life of the relationship. Worse, when we start a new relationship, these old connections are triggered and all the toxic emotions encysted within them can taint our new relationship.

Cords are not always bad. They do not all start out as nasty. In fact, they often begin with love and a feeling of safety and belonging—as between mothers and babies—or a strong sexual chemistry and attraction. It's only as time goes on that they might turn toxic. When this happens the cords actively prevent us from taking responsibility for what appear to be our own emotions. We become lost in the emotional run-off we share with other people. To get rid of unnecessary baggage and painful debris from a relationship—so we can interact free from the ties of the past—we need to clear the cord.

Before a cord can be cleared, though, we need to identify what we can readily own as our emotion and what might be coming from someone else.

Sometimes we feel we are merging with a partner or a close friend, losing ourselves. We might feel swamped in someone else's emotion, their pain or their anger. In such cases we need to see that this is their problem to process. We do not help them or ourselves by taking that emotion on board ourselves. Let it go, allow the other person to learn the lesson that comes with the situation, allow them to get stronger by handling it themselves.

Sometimes we take other people's stuff on board without realizing it. We can see how automatically this can happen even in an interaction that is not a close friendship or romantic relationship. A masseuse treating a patient bursts into tears, unable to bear the pain and sadness she can feel coming off her client's tense muscles. On later reflection, the client might recognize what she has been carrying unawares, and own the grief and pain as hers. The masseuse, however, needs a break to cleanse herself of her client's energy. She can do this by washing the length of her arms under cold running water for a couple of minutes while intentionally letting it go. This is not a toxic cord, but simply an example of how we "catch" other people's emotional energy and can think it is ours.

It's not only masseurs who experience this. A dentist talks about patients who come in with a hangover, and when they leave, they leave their headaches with the dentist. It's important if you work close to people in this way that after every session you have a routine way of cleansing the energy your clients and patients can leave with you. If you do not, your next client can end up with part of it, and your treatment is made less effective and even, at times, toxic. If the energy we pick up in this way feels uncomfortable or painful, we might also try to push it away from us or retreat from the emotional connection to protect ourselves. Unfortunately, this resistance merely makes it stick even more. The best idea is to let it flow through, knowing it will pass, and do whatever cleansing is needed. Nevertheless, this natural and normal energetic flow is not necessarily itself a toxic cord. The relationships in which a toxic cord forms are usually much more intense.

Chapter 2

Toxic relationships

So how do you know if you have cords to others in your life and if they are toxic? An energetic cord is like an open telephone line. It carries thoughts and emotions, usually unwanted, from one person to the other. Most of the time it's an unconscious transmission. We might be working away at our job, and suddenly feel a huge unexplained anger. Or a feeling of sadness, even depression, that can unexpectedly make us feel bleak and hopeless, which has no readily identifiable cause in the environment we are in at the time.

If we are sure one of our own sore points has not been triggered to cause this, we might find it originates in someone with whom we share an energetic cord. They are having a bad day, are angry at something and they push the energy of anger away from themselves and down it goes through the cord to us. This can happen in both directions, and we do it quite unconsciously.

Cord relationships in the people around you can show up in intriguing ways. Those linked by a cord will often use the same phrases, speech mannerisms or gestures. They might unconsciously turn up wearing the same colors or style of clothes on the same day, even when they have no prior knowledge of what the other is wearing. A friend's brother always seems to know when she needs a cheer-up phone call. Long-time friends or partners will often find one says what the other was thinking. With an elderly married couple I know, one often puts the kettle on just as the other thinks about making a cup of tea. Or she will call him to remind him to buy something at the shop and he has just bought it. While this is not a toxic connection, this kind of thought transference is quite often an indication of a cord.

A toxic cord is apparent when we let anxiety about a relationship keep us distracted from focusing on everyday life. Sometimes we feel we must behave in a way that conforms to what we believe are someone's expectations, so that all our interactions end up being in the same narrow emotional range. We might be convinced our partner is cheating, with no hard evidence. We might feel a sibling or friend dumps on us or drains us energetically. Perhaps we feel unable to escape a friend's distress, that somehow they "have a hold on us." The limiting way a parent sees us can end up being the way we see ourselves. Perhaps our boss feels we're not assertive enough, so we end up being not as assertive as we'd like. We might wish a relationship were more equal. Instead, it is one-sided and we're unable to balance it.

A toxic cord can make us feel trapped or restricted, or put us on a rollercoaster of intense emotional mood swings. All this can lead to self-destructive behavior such as wanting to wipe ourselves out with drugs or alcohol. Or we might react by acting out our frustration and unhappiness in ways that in turn affect our family and others.

There are often tangible signs when we have a toxic cord. The next time you suddenly hear the name of someone significant to you, or receive an unexpected phone call or message from them, observe where in your body you feel a reaction. You might feel a physical pain, like a stab in your heart, stomach or head. A cord can attach anywhere on our bodies. It's where we'll feel a tug, spasm, heaviness or ache when we think of the other person. Some of us literally feel the cord, a few might "see" them in the mind's eye or sense a subtle change in energy.

A cord is reactive, meaning that when we unconsciously receive energy in the form of unspoken emotional runoff, we react exactly as we would if someone had audibly provoked us. If someone close to us becomes powerfully resentful and we receive it through the cord, it resonates with, and provokes, our own store of resentment— about something else entirely. We end up feeling resentment with no clear cause. Anxiety has the same effect—where our own anxiety is keyed in like a tuning fork by someone else's worry. With a cord re- lationship, the transmission of that emotion through the cord causes a reaction within us that we are sometimes unable to connect to any obvious cause.

For example, if a mother is anxious, she can unintentionally push that anxiety onto her child throughout his childhood. As he grows up, and right through adulthood, he might in turn unconsciously feed his general anxieties back to her to gain a feeling of safety and calm. This off-loading of anxiety increases emotional tension in each of them.

We don't necessarily know that these unexplained feelings have come to us from another person. If it's a sudden feeling of anger, we might look for something in our immediate environment to explain why we are angry. Because what we are feeling is not logical or easily explained, the mind then seizes on something, or invents it, to make our anger more understandable. So, when we feel angry, we look around for something to focus that anger on. We find something someone has done in our environment that normally makes us angry and pin the blame on them. If we were to look at the situation a little more closely, we would realize that we were angry *beforehand*, and that whatever we focused on simply allowed us to vent this anger. We can gain much insight by asking ourselves what has really caused the anger—or any emotion—we are feeling.

Of course, there could be many other reasons, apart from a cord, that we suddenly feel anger—or any other emotion. Sometimes it may be our own insecurity, rather than our partner actually cheating, that makes us feel betrayed by someone we love. In every case we need discernment. Whatever emotional space we are in, we attract that to us. We then pick up and resonate with these emotions in others, including those strangers in crises on our television news.

Intense feelings with those we know have even more pull on us. There is a particular magnetism because they are so familiar. We can then be unconsciously pulled into a knee-jerk way of behaving or feeling whenever we think of them or encounter someone similar. So, we instantly like or dislike a stranger because they unconsciously remind us of a parent, boss or friend. In these situations we might discover that a cord to someone in our past—or present—keeps us tied to an old way of feeling or behaving.

Chapter 3

Am I in a toxic relationship or what?

BETRAYAL

When 25-year-old Talia was suddenly fired from her job in unfair circumstances she decided she needed some time away on her own. Her partner, Ben, worked at the same company and appeared fine with her going away for a month. She decided to tell no one where she was going, not even Ben, apart from a vague mention of another state on the opposite coast. To let anyone know anything further seemed to give away more than she had already lost. Besides, since Ben had not stood up for her when she was fired, she was not entirely sure that he was not somehow involved in her dismissal. Needing to clear her head of anger and confusion, Talia set off across the country and kept moving for a month. She hoped change would help her get some perspective on her recent difficulties and hopefully reinvent herself.

After three weeks of contact only with strangers, she had a

strange dream. She dreamed Ben was in bed with Angie, a girl they both knew. The dream was clear and unusually detailed, if a little weird. She saw their bed as a raft in a sea of long grass that swayed sensuously as though blown by the wind. Around them were many disembodied faces and translucent, headless bodies that glowed and floated in random motion. From a viewpoint somewhere above the bed, she distinctly heard Ben as he tenderly declared to Angie, "I love you, as you are now and as you are changing." Talia woke in chilled shock. Early in their relationship Ben had said exactly the same thing to her.

She called Ben twice that day but he wasn't answering his cell phone. The home phone kept ringing, the answering machine was not on. Two days later, she called again, this time to let Ben know she would be home a day earlier than she had thought. She sent a text to his cell phone as well. Still no answer. Anxiety grew in her until she arrived home at sunset.

The apartment they shared together was empty, but it was obvious that Ben had been entertaining. The bed was unmade, the sheets stained and rumpled. Candles had burned down into congealed pools and dripped down to the floor. Incense ash littered the top of the chest of drawers. Wine glasses with the remains of red wine stood on the bedside table. One was lipstick-smudged. A chiffon scarf that she did not recognize was draped over a lampshade. A bottle of scented massage oil—*her* massage oil—stood smeared and uncapped next to the glasses.

Distraught, Talia immediately got into her car and began to drive. Ben was still not answering his cell phone. She drove without knowing where she was going, her mind thrashing, needing to reconcile desolate conclusions. After half an hour she found herself in a part of the city where she had never been, in a cul-de-sac at the harbor's edge. She stopped the car in front of a house, her gaze on the lights of boats and the moon's reflection on the water. Her brain hurt. As she got out, her attention was drawn to a car in the driveway next to the house.

It was Ben's car.

Talia was stupefied, but it seemed entirely right to walk up to the front door and knock, her heart hammering at every step. She noticed as Angie opened the door that she was wearing a sarong. The girl's mouth dropped in utter surprise. Behind her in the hallway, Ben's voice called out, "Who is it?" When Angie did not reply he came up beside her, his eyes widening in shock at the sight of Talia. His next reaction twisted his mouth as he asked, "Have you been spying on me?"

Talia shook her head and pushed past them both, frowning, going the few feet straight to a bedroom which led off the hallway, its door open. It was the bed she had seen. On the floor was seagrass matting. Several painted theatrical masks hung on the walls and colorful diaphanous scarves draped the lampshades—which she recognized as the disembodied heads and headless bodies she had seen in her dream. She nodded, confirming what she already knew, and turned to face Ben and Angie who stood blinking and swallowing on the threshold. Ben was beginning to look thunderous.

Icily ignoring his growing anger, Talia said to Ben, "I don't care when you come to pick up your stuff from the apartment. You'll find a good deal of it on the front path whenever you get there." His eyes shifted. It looked as though he didn't know what to say. She turned to Angie and said, "You know when he said 'I love you as you are now and as you are changing'? Well, he said that to me, too.

Watch out." Talia walked out of the house and drove off without looking back.

Talia was perhaps only a little more psychic than the next person. From the beginning of their relationship she had intuitively known how Ben was feeling about things without his telling her, though she hadn't trusted her own knowledge. She was unaware at this stage that the connection between them was like a pipeline, an intense energetic cord that carried information to her about how he was feeling and what he was doing.

Emotions are energy, and they pass between us like electricity. In a way that was sometimes vague and sometimes very clear, Talia often knew what Ben was doing when they were apart. Right now, it was knowledge she really wished she had not received. For a cheating lover, an energetic cord is a dangerous thing. For the one cheated, it's a painful deliverer of truth. In cord relationships, not everyone gets dreams or images that flag a cheat, but every cord carries energy from one to the other. It simply depends on how aware we are of what this energy actually is. It is a level of awareness we can cultivate.

Though she was glad that she knew, Talia cycled between deep hurt and fury at Ben for the way in which he had betrayed her. The energetic cord continued to transmit unwanted images, emotions and information to her for some time after they split. If anything, the pain and unpleasantness intensified, making it harder to move on.

Ben compensated for his guilt and discomfort at being discovered with an outraged conviction that Talia had been spying on him. When she told him about her dream and the fact that she had been away until a few hours before she knocked on Angie's door, he didn't believe her and ended the conversation in a fury. Once alone, he used this to justify blaming her and fanned it into hatred, fed by countless unspoken irritations from earlier in their relationship. Volatile emotions transmitted straight through the cord in angry bursts to Talia. In turn, Talia's rage, grief and pain were sent back along the cord to Ben. Neither of them knew what was happening as they went through this painful process. Each thought the emotions they were receiving from the other were their own. While they might have been able to discharge these emotions if they were their own, they could do nothing to resolve emotions that originated in someone else.

DESPERATE AND DUMPED

Secure as a mollusk on a sea-tide rock, Oliver felt his four-year relationship with Julie was perfectly fine. One day, without knowing why, he picked up her phone and checked the messages she had saved. What he found unhinged all his illusions of safety.

The tiny, telltale screen displayed an intimate message from one of her work colleagues referring to their passionate affair. Shocked and disbelieving, he confronted her, but all Julie could say was that she had become close to her friend Justin without meaning anything to happen. She concluded that Justin simply needed her more than Oliver did. She seemed to think this explanation was sufficient.

Three weeks of awkward, incomplete conversations and painful silences followed. Julie was often at Justin's for days at a time. Oliver didn't want to let her go. He couldn't believe it was ending this way. To add to the confusion, Julie was acting like a different person. As long as he had known her she had been fragile, suffering numerous phobias and anxieties, while he'd always provided calm support and encouragement. Now she was more independent and outgoing than he'd ever known her to be; taking on a supportive role to Justin, who was evidently needy and insecure.

Oliver was baffled as well as devastated when Julie said she knew he was strong and that he'd be fine, whereas Justin could not cope without her. Oliver could not understand how little she seemed actually to know him, but he was unaware that he had never shown himself fully to her. As a typical Rescuer Character,[1] he had molded himself to fit Julie's needs as he perceived them and had only seen in her what he wanted to see. He had needed her to be weak so that he could be strong.

When Julie finally left, Oliver grew suicidally depressed. He lost all motivation for work, stalking her obsessively—physically and online. He nearly succeeded in an attempt to take his own life and spent some time in a psychiatric hospital. Eventually he was well enough to take a job on contract in another country. A series of desultory affairs led nowhere. His heart pined for Julie, who seemed to have forgotten all about him.

Two years later, with his therapist, he realized that when he was stalking her—tracking her social activity online—he had needed to continue hurting himself to convince himself there was no hope. He also realized that much of the time he was behaving in a way that was futilely designed for Julie's attention, approval and benefit, and not the way he wanted to be.

Oliver's therapy then focused on what was stopping him moving on. He felt he was still attached to Julie though he was not clear how. It was more than just missing her. Friends told him he needed to cut the umbilical cord. As Oliver reflected on this in a therapy session, he felt it tangibly as something attached to his solar plexus, and that "something" came through this to him, or from him to her. In fact, whenever he thought of Julie, his diaphragm went into a painful spasm.

At this stage Oliver couldn't identify what he was feeling as actually coming from her. Perhaps there was a sense of rejection, but Oliver wasn't sure whether he was projecting or imagining this.

It was difficult for Oliver to see or feel what vibe was coming from Julie because he had never really known who Julie was. He couldn't even describe what her energy was like because, in the codependent relationship they had, their energies had merged and blurred. It's also why, unlike Talia with Ben, Oliver was unaware that Julie was cheating, because he had become lost in her needs. Neither of them was seeing the other as they truly were but had fitted their fantasies conveniently over each other. While Julie had been fragile and clinging in her relationship with Oliver, he had derived great comfort from being needed. Oliver knew he was far from strong or emotionally independent but he could be that way for Julie. When Julie had been attracted by Justin's need, she had responded in a Rescuer role that had previously been filled by Oliver for her. For the moment she was happier being supportive, though her relationship with Justin was just as codependent as with Oliver.

As his therapy progressed, Oliver began to feel what was in the cord, exactly how it affected him and to get glimpses of what it transmitted in the way of energy or emotions from Julie. He described the sluggish, heavy energy lining his pelvis where he felt the cord attach to his body. It made him feel helpless and hopeless, and when he first tuned in to it he felt an initial surge of panic that passed so quickly he almost missed it. He now recognized it as what he had "handled" all through his relationship with Julie. She had off-loaded this unwanted energy on to him, while Oliver had tacitly agreed to take it from her and become her emotional garbage bin. In his Nice Guy Character, he had been quite happy to do this for her, though they never spoke of it. If he thought of it at all, it was in the realm of helping her. In turn, when Julie met Justin she quickly realized that being needed, instead of needy, made her feel useful, stronger and happier. She had shed her old Needy Character like a hermit crab seeking the bigger shell of a Provider/Carer Character.

Oliver was only now becoming aware of what he had unconsciously agreed to, and the unhealthy basis of their relationship. Though much of the bad feeling he was left with after the breakup was about being deceived so completely by someone he trusted, he was slightly heartened when he realized that on an unconscious level he had actually felt some change in her. It had prompted him, uncharacteristically, to check her phone. Logically, he thought that if he already had this intuitive ability, albeit undeveloped, he could probably cultivate it and use it to become more aware of what was going on in his life in general. He hoped he would never be blindsided like that again.

As Oliver explored the heavy feeling in his pelvis, he initially thought of it as an old, residual energy from Julie. To his surprise he realized he was still sending emotional run-off to her along the cord and even though he was now on the other side of the world, the cord stretched elastically as though distance was irrelevant. Most of it had been completely unconscious until recently, but he could feel that all his neediness, his sense of abandonment and the resulting pain was still pulsing out through the cord to Julie. He could now sense clearly how this flow of emotion from him was being rejected by her. In his inner eye he saw the cord as a festering toxic mass of energy feeding on itself and draining his vitality. It was stopping him making new lasting relationships, dampening his will and souring his motivation. So toxic had this connection between them become that it had contaminated his entire energy field, leaving him feeling that nothing mattered anymore.

It wasn't until Oliver had the cord cleared that he felt free, more himself than he had ever felt. He was now able to take responsibility for his own emotions and energy in a way he had never been able to before.

On the other side of the world, Julie had no idea what he was doing, since they were no longer in direct contact. A clearing of an energetic cord to an old relationship was probably not something she had thought about. It's common, however, that after a cord clearing, the person on the other end feels something in a vague sort of way, even if they don't know anything about it. Sometimes the person on the other end will feel, as though on a whim, the need to renew contact. Sometimes they feel inexplicably freer.

At this stage, Oliver no longer wanted to reconnect with Julie on any level. Interestingly, a few weeks later he caught up with a friend from his old hometown who told him that Julie's relationship with Justin had broken up. Oliver realized the breakup occurred only a few days after he had had the cord cleared. In fact, Julie had cried on the friend's shoulder in the old needy and anxious way. Hearing this, Oliver couldn't help but feel a little stab of righteous pleasure that she was experiencing something of what he had suffered for so long.

But when he brought this development to his therapy session, he looked at it more deeply. He knew that after he and Julie had split, the heavy energy he had always felt from her and the hopelessness it carried had not disappeared but had continued to flow to him. When the cord was cleared, the means by which she had off-loaded this onto Oliver was gone. On the other hand, Justin certainly couldn't handle her "stuff." It was no wonder that Julie and Justin had split as well.

Oliver's friend knew how attached he'd been to Julie and asked him if he would now go back home. It was then that Oliver realized he was no longer interested in a codependent relationship. He had a new life. He was free.

Chapter 4

Parents and children

WHEN ATTACHMENTS WORK FOR US

In the building of healthy human beings, attachment is far from a bad thing. A close connection between infants and their parents and other caregivers creates happier, more independent children who cope well with frustrations and obstacles and who have confidence in themselves and trust in those around them. However, when very young children do not feel this secure connection to their parents or a carer early in their lives, it can lead to a lifetime of unhealthy attachments attempting to make up for the deficiency.[2]

When a child has a safe and secure base they will begin to explore their environment. It's a natural curiosity essential for survival that we can see play out in any documentary on the life cycle of mammals, from wolves to whales. If in this exploration something threatens a young animal—or a child—they will naturally seek the safety of mother once more. The more welcoming the mother is, the more safety a child feels to begin the next exploration. The repetition of this experience builds security in the child and overlaps into confidence in social relationships with people other than just their mother. Secure attachment has been linked in studies to the ability of a child to cope well with highly stressful events at any age to adulthood.

"Securely attached" children are so called because they have experienced a reliably secure relationship from the start. They develop social skills by being confident enough to leave mom's side to play with other children, knowing she will be there when they need her. They learn empathy through mirroring what they see in their mothers' faces and, through that, consideration for others. This happy outcome depends on whether their parents are emotionally and physically available, and if they respond without undue panic when, for example, an infant has colic or a toddler hurts himself. If a mother or a father is generally calm, a child will learn to be calm, too.

We can tell if our child is securely attached or not in how they handle being left in a strange situation such as preschool.[3] When Josephine brought her little daughter Sophie into preschool for the first time, both of them were feeling a bit nervous. It was all so new. Josephine stayed for a little while to make sure Sophie was okay, told her smilingly she would be back soon and was heading out the door just as Sophie began a loud wail. The teacher holding Sophie's hand immediately knelt down and comforted her, waving to Mommy. Josephine waited out of sight, but not earshot, and soon heard Sophie's wailing stop, her attention distracted by something the teacher was showing her. While preschool was a very unfamiliar place at first, Sophie was a securely attached child who quickly learned that it was fun. There were playmates, the teachers were caring, and Mom or Dad were always there at the end of the day to pick her up with lots of cuddles and take her home. After this first time, Sophie rarely made any fuss when being left at preschool.

Josephine is sensitively attuned to her child. She was consistently responsive to Sophie's needs from birth to around the age of two, after which she began to gradually and gently allow her daughter to experience her mother not always attending to her every need.

Sophie's later development will be based on her early secure attachment. In the normal way of things, Sophie found preschool frightening because it is a huge transition for a young child, and to ease the strangeness she sucked her thumb, as other children might carry a teddy bear or comforter. Knowing that she could still get love and care from her parents, she soon gained confidence when they were absent and she was at preschool. This growing confidence underpinned her later explorations and experiences and she also eventually and quite naturally outgrew her thumb sucking.

OUR FIRST CORDS

In many cases our first cord begins in the womb, exactly like the umbilical cord, though in energy form. Sometimes it forms before conception. On occasion, using subtle vision, I have seen one or a number of babies wanting to be born hovering above the chosen mother's energy field. Once conception has occurred, an energetic cord links the incoming spirit to the fetal body within the womb.

The spirit of the baby comes and goes for quite long periods during pregnancy. It often floats within their mother's astral body, attached by a cord that resembles the umbilical cord. This can have the effect of augmenting the light and space of the mother's aura in an extraordinary way. The connection between the baby's physical body and their subtle bodies seems to allow much more elasticity of movement at this age, with the spirit not yet restricted inside the physical body.

While the baby's physical body sleeps, the incoming being travels through spiritual worlds wholly awake and immersed in unconditional love. Through the baby's cord, many mothers become more intuitive and psychically sensitive at this time. Some mothers might develop telepathic abilities or have dreams that accurately show the future. Their perception can deepen to the point where they can see subtle energies such as auras. Their empathy deepens, in tune with the unconditional love of spiritual connection. Their emotions are heightened by hormones at the same time. This can mean some wildly alternating cycles of serenity and intense emotional reaction.

Just as the baby's physical body is affected by their mother's physical condition, their subtle bodies are under the influence of their mother's emotions during the pregnancy and for some time after birth. These emotions can impact deeply on their energy field, so that a child will react to their mother's triggered emotions as though they are their own. It can be overwhelming. The emotional triggers restimulate the pain of what in Sanskrit is called a samskara. It's an unresolved emotional wound from the past, deeply embedded in the astral body, which conditions us to react in certain predictable ways.

A growing child gradually edges out of their mother's astral body and influence. At some stage, the two energy fields separate, indicating the child's increasing individuality. If they don't, the overlap contributes to an unhealthy energetic cord that prevents the child maturing. Inevitably, we form partnerships as adults that mimic those immature relationships we had with our parents. We echo their samskaric reactions to people and situations and might unconsciously agree to less personal space than we should have, in a defensive attempt to make ourselves smaller and less visible.

We are attracted to our parents for certain qualities of their personality that we also need to learn, model or transcend. Put simply, we are born to parents who will teach us, by example, what to do and what not to do. While our lower, instinctual self is hardwired to avoid pain and discomfort and would never choose abusive or neglectful parents, our wise Higher Self sees a larger picture and helps draw to us what we need to progress. Like it or not, most of us change only when it's too painful or uncomfortable to remain as we are.

As infants and children our focus is on survival—what we have to do to get love and affection, protection and approval, to please parents and teachers—because without these we cannot grow healthily. As adults we can hopefully choose more consciously how we want to be and act. By this stage we have more information, more wisdom and greater resources for long-term well-being and independence. When our parents model for us what we feel is bad parenting, this doesn't mean that we lose our Higher Self knowing of the right way to be. As very young children we might have wondered what we had done wrong, when looking back as adults we can see it was our parents' inabilities—intentional or not. Rather than blame the one on whom they depend for love and nurturing, children will often blame themselves for their parents' deficiencies.

Discovering that we did not receive the best parenting can make us shrink from the thought of becoming parents ourselves. How can we give unconditional love to our own child if we believe we never received it? Is there any way we can reconnect with a source of unconditional love for ourselves, despite our parents' failure?

Of course there is.

We can tune in to what we needed as a child. Perhaps a particular event or situation comes to mind, a time of sadness or loss, of feeling lost, or inadequate, or hopeless. At the same time as seeing how our parents failed, we can see what they should have done, and what we now as a responsive adult would do instead for that child. We would listen and hold that child in complete acceptance until they feel safe, warm, loved.

In some cases of terrible abuse and neglect, the adult survivor has little idea what the child they were needed, because the sense of self is so damaged. They might have difficulty relating to any child, including their own inner child, who still feels abandoned and needy, buried under a scaffolding of defenses. What a more fortunate child has affirmed in a close, secure parent-child relationship has never been learned. Sometimes this needs to be gently learned in the safety of therapy. It's a process of becoming wholehearted.

For most of us, though, it is a profound discovery that even if our parents failed us, we are not irrevocably broken. We can use this Higher Self knowledge to re-parent ourselves, by nurturing ourselves and giving ourselves the loving care we lacked during childhood. We can reconnect to a sense of the unconditional love of spirit from which we came and which is our true home. It becomes a joy to take responsibility for our own lives, and whether our parents failed us or not, to learn the lesson of truly valuing ourselves as we are. The end result is so empowering we may wonder why we never did it earlier.

MOTHER-DAUGHTER WARS

Nights were bleak for Jillian, whose 16-year-old daughter, Natasha, had run away for the third time in 18 months. Worrying about Natasha's risky behavior involving drugs, alcohol and sex was a full-time occupation. Making her mother anxious was Natasha's.

Jillian knew Natasha was playing a vicious remote control game. Try as she might, she was unable to detach enough to stop the worry. Her fear sparked terrors in her mind and rationality vanished. In Jillian's anxious mind, images flashed of Natasha dead in a gutter with a needle in her arm, Natasha being gang-raped, beaten up by vicious street thugs and left to die, kidnapped by sex traffickers or black-market organ harvesters. Natasha, gone forever. Each scene hit with what felt like physical impact and sweat poured from her, banishing sleep.

Jillian would hold back as long as she could, then begin the well-worn round of calling hospitals. Police were used to hearing her strained, tearful voice in early morning hours. Her anger at what Natasha was doing made her feel strong for short periods, until she collapzed into dread once more. She was helpless to prevent the scenes unreeling in her mind. At such times she felt her energy shrink while around her the air grew cold. She felt alone and sad, alternating between blaming Natasha and blaming herself.

At the other end, young Natasha felt the acrid clutch of her mother's panic and grief around her own ribcage, and shoved a wall of angry rejection back as hard as she could. Jillian's reproachful internalized voice was persistent and pitiful in her ear. The girl brought down a heavy curtain of suppression to ignore and deny feelings of guilt. It forced her into ever more extreme behavior in attempts to free herself from her emotional entanglement with her mother. Natasha felt as though a dark, enormous grasping hand, her mother's, was clutching her from head to toe and squeezing mercilessly. Sometimes she could hardly breathe.

Natasha felt that her whole life had been defined by a war with her mother. All Jillian had to do was sniff at something Natasha said, or raise an eyebrow with pursed mouth, and Natasha would immediately go into meltdown with an incandescent fury that took her over and caused her to smash whatever was nearby. On the other hand, Natasha's scornful grimaces, automatic frowns and angry flounces before she disappeared in a mess of breakages made Jillian walk on eggshells whenever they were together. Rational communication had long seemed impossible, yet Jillian persisted on the basis of what she believed a mother-daughter relationship *should* be. In the same vein, she was constantly disappointed to the point of heartbreak whenever Natasha behaved as a daughter shouldn't.

Running away had failed before for Natasha and it wasn't working this time either. Though there was the illusion of being free to do whatever she wanted, she was still behaving in extremes—as though her mother could see what she was doing and be hurt by it. Natasha was daring God, or her mother, to punish or stop her. In fact, the further away she got geographically, the more her mother's disapproval and sadness seemed to crush her and the angrier she herself became.

When Jillian thought about when it had all begun, it seemed Natasha's switch from being an adorable, smart, talented youngster occurred at around the age of 12. At puberty, Natasha began hiding what she was doing from her mother. Jillian felt increasingly shut out. One day, tidying her daughter's bedroom, she found and read Natasha's diary. She was horrified. Disastrously, she confronted her daughter with what she had read there. Natasha withdrew in fury and the next day "borrowed" some tools from the school wood workshop to install a padlock on her door.

Jillian pleaded with her to tell her the truth about what she was doing. Natasha scornfully pointed out that she had learned how to lie from her mother and that Jillian's supposedly secret drinking habit was the real reason her father had left them. Natasha's lying was an attempt to gain more space of her own, to keep her mother out. To the girl, the more her mother knew about her, the more power Jillian had over her. Running away was simply a more extreme attempt at a solution. She felt her mother had invaded every part of her life.

Jillian and Natasha were locked into compulsive and reactive behavior, dependent on what the other did. The emotions of one resonated with and amplified the other's, back and forth until neither of them could tell whose emotions they were actually feeling.

What they were experiencing was the toxic connection of an energetic cord. It bound them as surely to each other as the umbilical cord that had once nourished Natasha in the safety of Jillian's womb. Somewhere along the line it had stopped being healthy. Now, it was a hate-filled, painful attachment that depleted each of them and would not let go.

ATTACHMENTS FORMED BEFORE BIRTH

I suspect many parents vow they will never treat their kids the way their parents treated them, only to recoil in horror when they find themselves doing the same thing to their own children. During our lives, to a greater or lesser degree, we project variations of the issues we had with our parents onto every relationship. As depressing as this may seem, there's no point in condemning ourselves for falling into the same traps over and over again. On the one hand, our samskaric wounds are drawing to us more of the same energy. At the same time, our Higher Self is giving us the chance to resolve those issues in a slightly easier or, at least, different frame so we can evolve beyond that old conditioning.

So why can't we just decide to be different? If we want to understand why it is so difficult to detach from these old conditionings, Albert Einstein explained it when he said that no problem can be solved by the same level of consciousness that created it. The level of consciousness that creates the problem of painful attachment is a depth of unmet need that would rather have any connection than be alone. If we are in desperate need we are rarely able to detach from that need and see a better way to provide for ourselves. It's like being stuck up to the waist in a muddy marsh, trying to see the way out. All we can see is low scrub, more water and treacherous mud, and all the time we feel ourselves sinking deeper and deeper the more we struggle to get out. We might be able to see better if we could only crawl out onto dry land. We might be able to see further, to discover the path to safety, if we could climb a tree. Then we see a plane flying high above us. If only we were in that plane. We would be able to see the treacherous marsh and the safe areas in the surrounding countryside. The mind that is flying in the plane would see solutions, the way out. In fact, the mind that is flying in the plane would never get into the marsh in the first place.

The truth is, human beings are conscious on many levels. We are spiritual beings clad in physical bodies, more often than not in mud or struggling through a marsh. If we wade long enough in muddy wetlands we might forget there is any other way to be. In meditation, however, we can see that our true natural perspective is way above the struggle of the marsh, as though we were in that plane flying overhead. We can experience the all-encompassing and sublime connectedness of spirit. There is a sense of belonging in which we are an essential part of all creation. An infant in the womb is still connected to this amazing experience, having so recently come from it, and yet their awareness is no longer just of spirit worlds, but impacted by the much heavier energetic world of the physical body and matter. It can be a very confusing experience.

An unborn infant is immersed in the energy field of their mother and becomes imprinted with her emotions, thoughts and energy. Now, the infant is in the mud. Nothing in this world equates to the sense of infinite and eternal connection and belonging we have felt in spirit. The unconditional love of a mother comes close, but the much heavier energy of our conditioned human emotions makes the memory of frictionless spiritual connection rapidly fade.

A baby in the womb is cocooned within their mother's etheric energy field—the subtle body that contains her life force and responds to vibrations in the environment. We can feel the etheric body through subtle sensations—such as the shivers we get when we say someone is "walking over our grave." Our etheric life force is like electricity—and transmits in much the same way whether we are in the womb within our mother's energy field, or physically separated by distance, great or small.

An unborn infant is similarly immersed in the thoughts and emotions of their mother's astral body for their entire gestation. Unlike the etheric body, which is close to the physical in shape, the astral body is more like an ovoid field of energy at the core of which is our physical body. It usually extends for up to a yard from the skin and transmits thoughts, emotions and ideas, as well as catching these from others.

A mother can feel an extraordinary connection to her unborn baby, even a sense of the amazing being who is in the process of incarnating. She can tune in to how the baby is feeling within her

The Subtle Bodies

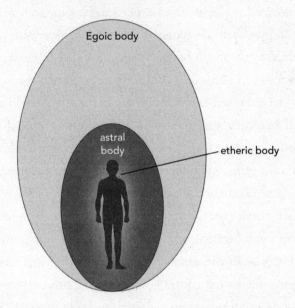

An out-of-scale representation of the subtle bodies. Egoic (outer oval). astral (smaller oval) and etheric (extending out from the human form).

through her subtle bodies. She might feel, for example, the extraordinary nurturing light that surrounds every fetus. She might also feel the baby's increasing physical discomfort as they grow and available space decreases. She might become aware that any tension, anxiety or anger she feels, as well as an enveloping love, also affect the baby. This is something that's likely to continue after birth.

Immersed in the energy field of their mother throughout a pregnancy, a baby feels everything she feels by default, without understanding it or having any way of distinguishing between their own emotional state and what their mother is feeling.

Most pregnant women are subject to a bewildering cascade of intense, hormonally generated emotions—everything from a blissful kind of happy-as-a-clam contentment to strong convictions that the baby will be born with two heads. Often we have no clue as to why we are feeling what we are feeling so intensely at that particular time. If you are a mother, for the baby's sake it's a good idea to remain as calm as you can, but don't worry too much if you get hormonal flashes of emotion. It's normal and human. We survived our mother's pregnancy, more or less. Let your emotions run their course without suppressing them. Feel them, express them—responsibly, safely—and move on. It's a handy habit to cultivate and to model for our children as they grow. It also leaves a mother-to-be freer to sense how her baby is doing in the womb if she is not worrying about—or suppressing—her own emotions.

If a pregnant woman rarely feels her unborn baby's psychic or emotional presence, or has no sense of the new consciousness within her, it may be because she's too immersed in her own emotional reactions. Or possibly she's tuning in at a time when the baby is traveling in spirit, out of their fetal body.

In the womb babies spend much of their time asleep, especially early in the pregnancy. Linked by an energetic cord to their embryonic body, the baby's spirit moves freely between the physical and spiritual worlds. The fact that their physical body is within their mother's energy field for the months of pregnancy means the baby automatically has a cord with their mother.

On occasion, an existing cord between partners allows a father also to have pregnancy symptoms, including back pain, tiredness, weight gain and even morning sickness, in what is commonly known as Couvade syndrome or male sympathetic pregnancy.[4] Men who experience these symptoms report feeling closer to their partners and to their unborn child, but they don't need to suffer through their wife's pregnancy to connect to a child when it is born. The bonds that form between fathers and their newborns can be just as loving and protective as between mothers and their infants.

As a means of connecting to other consciousnesses, we are actually used to cords. Although the psychic cords that are the subject of this book are astral-etheric in composition, and often toxic, their basic structure is similar to our Egoic connection to our higher selves, from whom we receive subtle information throughout our lives, but where the energy and perception is far clearer. Sometimes called the Column of Spirit,[5] this stretches vertically up from the crown of our heads. It is a device we can cultivate in meditation by intention and aspiration. Through it we can receive grace, which often feels like a very subtle shower of light or energy; exhilarating, reviving and refreshing. It is the pathway through which our Higher Ego and our Archetype can land, and through it we can connect with the limitless presence and consciousness of vast spiritual beings.[6]

As above, so below. The Column of Spirit can be a conduit of spiritual nourishment just as the umbilical cord provides physical nourishment for a baby in the womb.

In cords that form before conception, we are drawn as though by magnetic attraction to the energy field of our mother. This continues until we are mature and independent enough not to need it, or until it is cleared.

When a baby is born, the energetic cord they have with their mother remains after the umbilical cord is cut. It continues to nurture the child and can also let the mother know instantly how her child is feeling at any moment. Depending on how aware she is, she can know if her child is happy or not, if their crying is distress or just discomfort or, if they are apart, if her child is safe or in danger.

While this connection is important for parents and their babies, many mothers or fathers end up too close to their babies and wires get crossed. Then instead of helping us, our connection creates confusion because we're no longer clear about what we're feeling, as opposed to what baby is feeling. Or we're too anxious about being good parents to trust our intuition. Here's where it is important to be *differentiated*—to see ourselves as individuals separate to other individuals. This space between us makes it far easier to discern the difference between our own energetic/emotional state and that of our babies. It doesn't make us less loving to allow space in this way—in fact it enables us to know more clearly what baby needs, and no less important, what we need as well. And when we are differentiated adults, we can put our baby's needs first for that all-important and necessary early period. When we are not differentiated, it generally means our own needs as infants have not been met, and we are less able as adults to make our baby's needs a priority as a result.

Knowing what the baby needs includes being aware of when to begin to detach—by tiny degrees at first, when the child is around two years of age. It's a matter of being sensitively attuned to the child's requirements for comfort, sleep and nourishment as well as their growing need to explore their environment and return to the safe nearness of their parents.

CHECKING OUR CORDS

Long after her breakup with Ben, Talia married and had a little boy who plunged her life into magical, joy-filled chaos. One day Talia was working in the kitchen while Matthew, not yet one year old, crawled around in the child-safe area nearby. She didn't realize someone had left the childproof gate open until a sharp picture flashed urgently into her brain. She ran immediately to the veranda, where a gleeful Matthew was sitting perched on the top step. His floor-level view of the five steps down to the garden was identical to the image that had flashed in her head. Along with the image was a telepathic communication, a curious and excited, "What is this?" Until he learned to speak, Matthew used this form of communication without exception.

Talia was immensely relieved that she'd received the message in time to save her son from possible hurt. She realized this was an exploration he needed, but she couldn't safely let him explore the steps on his own. She responded to his telepathic question with a spoken answer that echoed his excitement. "Let's learn about gravity, Matti," and smiled. She lifted Matti and maintained smiling eye contact with him. Gently she bumped him down each step on his bottom, until he was on the garden path. Despite the last "bump" being intentionally a little harder than the others, Matti gurgled and beamed.

After this incident, when Talia was busy and Matti was playing nearby, she often received images from him accompanied by a variety of excited telepathic comments or questions such as, "What is this?" "Is this safe?" or "Look at me!" and "This is fun!" Talia would check that he was safe, make the appropriate response, and he would continue until the next discovery or he returned for a hug. If the image was worrying—such as the time he learned to unlatch the garden gate and wandered out toward the road—Talia learned to respond instantly with a telepathic "Matti, stop!" message. On that occasion she had been gardening with her back to him, and whipped around to see him standing calmly next to the road, smiling and waiting for her. As she rushed toward him, she was careful not to show alarm, but praised him for stopping where it was safe.

Interestingly, mother and son got so good at this telepathic communication that Matti was slow to learn to speak. Talia would receive his message, such as "I want a drink of juice," as a clear picture of his sippy cup and the flavor of orange juice somehow conveyed at the same time. Thinking ahead, Talia worried that Matti might run into a few problems at preschool if he thought everyone would know what he wanted without having to say it out loud. So, when he sent her his telepathic requests, she would smile and repeat the message out loud, "Do you want orange juice?" He would nod and she would wait. "Say it out loud, Matti," she encouraged him, and when he did she praised him and gave him his juice. Talia patiently did this over and over again, until he began, not without irritation, to speak when he wanted to communicate.

As Matti and her later-born children grew, there were other occasions when Talia relied on their cord connections to let her know if they were safe when she couldn't actually see them. Checking them every now and then, she didn't feel the cords were toxic, but she did wonder at times whether she needed to cut them for her children's greater benefit. It's a healthy, responsible thing for any parent to consider at regular points in their children's upbringing whether their cords have become toxic.

Chapter 5

Unhealthy family connections

MOMMY'S BOY

Rhonda's husband was a merchant seaman, frequently away for months at a time from his wife and their toddler, Damien. Rhonda was always worried that her son might hurt himself if she let him out of her sight or if he was too adventurous. If Damien was pulling himself up onto furniture, Rhonda would panic and scream at him to stop because he would fall. Alarmed at the anxious tone in his mother's voice, Damien would begin to cry and, of course, fall on his bottom. Rhonda would then clasp him to her, "Mommy is here. Mommy will always be here and will never let you get hurt!" A startled Damien would feel his mother's distress and continue to cry for much longer than he might have done if left to his own explorations.

As time went on, whenever Damien's father was away, the little boy shared Rhonda's bed because he was too anxious to sleep on his own—but sometimes also because Rhonda was frightened or missing her husband. Even more disturbing, by the time Damien was nine things hadn't changed.

Once, out shopping with his mother, the young Damien ran ahead on the path to the traffic lights, jumping up and down there and looking back excitedly at his mother. When Rhonda caught up to him she hit him solidly across the back of the head, yelling at him furiously to never do that again. Not trusting her son to stop before rushing out in traffic, even though he had not, her fright was expressed in anger. Meanwhile Damien began a shocked wail, unaware of what he had done that warranted being hit so hard.

By the time he reached puberty, Rhonda's anxiety had turned Damien into a pale, overweight and clingy child. Mother and son were too fused together to feel any separation between them and neither could think of Damien acting independently. To become aware of a cord, there needs to be a degree of separation for either person to feel the toxic connection. Damien was too enmeshed in his mother's energy to feel the difference between his own emotions and his mother's.

It was never Rhonda's intention to create a Mommy's Boy. Like most parents she was simply doing the best she could with what she knew. She didn't see her caring for Damien as overprotectiveness, nor her compulsive control as oppressive. She had no idea she was doing this to compensate for her own neediness. Because Rhonda had not addressed and overcome her own anxieties, she was bequeathing them to Damien, leaving him feeling powerless and with no personal space. It was exactly how Rhonda had felt with her own mother, but she had no idea it could be any different.

From the beginning, Rhonda laid her own anxieties onto her child whether or not there was cause. As he grew, she unconsciously made him responsible for her happiness and well-being, while at the same time finding him a constant disappointment. It was far too great a burden for anyone to bear, and it ruined Damien. Years later she could manipulate him into feeling guilty simply with a heavy pause on the telephone line. In his 40s, he'd never had a romantic relationship with a woman. He felt far safer relating emotionally, and responding sexually, to adolescent boys. Damien knew his mother's hate-filled attitude toward this and so never let her, or the religious community in which he found refuge, know his secret, shame-tinged attraction. In fact, having never in his life felt her approval, no matter what, he projected disapproval onto everyone whom he felt had authority over him.

We might not always know we have an unhealthy attachment to our child, especially if we're a first-time mother. It's easier to see it in others. For example, if I'm sitting on a bus opposite a baby in a stroller I usually make very gentle eye contact with the infant. Connecting telepathically with a tiny baby is often an experience of blazing joy and mutual fun. There's a sparkling electric transmission as the baby connects, a pure glee along with a gurgling laugh and shining eyes that goes back and forth.

If the baby's mother is insecure, fearful or needy, she will interrupt this connection as though protecting her child from something dangerous. She'll pick the child up and hold them close, directing their attention to herself. This can be an indication of an unhealthy cord connection. When I meet a baby with sad, fearful or dull eyes and a lack of interest in connecting with anyone but their mom, with whom it's an obviously anxious interchange, it's often a sign of an unhealthy attachment.

It's important not to blame the mother for this. No mother wishes to disable her child emotionally. Her fear of losing the connection to her baby, her suspicion and discomfort, are in most cases to do with her own past, her own deficient parenting. It's normal to feel vulnerable when our own needs have not been met and we are expected to supply the needs of our children. When a mother can recognize her own anxiety, it helps to know that she can overcome it by focusing on what her child needs now, despite the fears based in her own past. It's not her fault, but it's within her power to change it.

Mothers who are relaxed and secure enough within themselves allow their babies to make connections with trusted other people in a natural way. They allow their toddlers to curiously explore the world outside their relationship with Mom, without anxiety. When exploring, a child will often look back at Mom for reassurance or to share their enjoyment. In smiling and enjoying their child's play at a distance, these mothers are reinforcing that caregiving relationship without interfering or distancing themselves. Equally comfortably, they also welcome their child back into their arms when the child has had enough of experiencing the world outside.

Overattentiveness—such as when mothers continue attending to their children even after they no longer need it—creates unrealistic expectations in children. Interestingly, the kind of parenting that avoids the insecurity that forms the basis for toxic attachments reflects a realistic approach, and is called "good enough mothering."[7] These mothers, fathers and carers allow the child to learn how to interact in the world and develop independence at their own pace. They set a platform for an emotionally healthy, sociable child who is engaged with life and does not love them less, but often more.

If you are a mother of a young child, notice your own emotions when your child wanders off to explore, and when they come back after their adventure. If you feel anxious when your child leaves your side, or when they return for a reassuring hug, know that it's very normal—most parents will feel this at some stage to varying degrees. However, if it is an unhealthy attachment, your child will be affected. You will see them watching you constantly with a degree of anxiety to see whether you are okay with what they are doing, and the child will change their response accordingly. It's a sign of a need to work on yourself and your own insecurities before you inadvertently imprint them on your child. In the words of the Circle of Security Project, a form of training for parents of toddlers, children need a parent to be "always bigger, stronger, wiser and kind. Where possible, a parent should follow a child's lead. Whenever necessary, a parent should take charge."[8]

Sometimes, when one parent is unhealthily attached, their partner can offer some balance from a less attached viewpoint. Obviously, a sensitively worded observation, and not criticism, is called for here. In the following story, Charlotte's husband, Jack, found a novel way of showing Charlotte what was behind their toddler's behavior.

In the middle of the "terrible twos" young Finn cried, had frequent tantrums and whined persistently until his mother, Charlotte, who had a new baby as well, was utterly worn down and at her wits' end. She just didn't know what to do. One day, Finn's father Jack set up the video camera and left the room to record what happened after Charlotte had put the toddler in the Time Out corner. He wailed for a while, as Charlotte gritted her teeth and carried on trying to feed the new baby in another room nearby. After a few minutes, Finn grew quiet. Hearing silence, Charlotte got up and peeped to see if he was okay. He was fine, engrossed in playing, until he looked up to see his mum, upon which his face instantly became tragic and he began to wail again. Charlotte immediately ducked back into the baby's room without saying anything. Finn's wailing continued for another few minutes and tapered off again. Each time his mother checked on him, the video recording showed Finn launching into what was evidently designed to be a heartbreaking wail once more.

It took the video to show Charlotte how Finn was watching for her reaction, and that she was being manipulated by the distress her son was putting on for her benefit. As a result, Charlotte and Jack were able to understand how they were inadvertently contributing to their son's behavior and adjusted their parenting. They began by sharing with him what they felt might be the reasons why he was upset, so he had the language to tell them instead of acting out—for example, "You're tired, Finn, and it's making you grumpy." They rewarded him whenever he asked in a normal tone of voice for what he needed and praised him every time he was more in control of himself, while making sure they allowed Finn to express normal emotions. It was equally a learning phase for Jack and Charlotte, who wished above all to be good parents to their children. They learned that, as parents, helping our children not to be clingy, fearful or anxious makes parenthood so much more satisfying and fun.

SEPARATION ANXIETY AND INTIMACY ISSUES

Of course, the ideal of secure attachment and a sensitively attuned parent is often not the case. If a mother is anxious on her child's venturing out to explore, the child feels mom's anxiety through the cord as though it is their own.

This was the case with Sheila and Todd, who felt how uncomfortable it made his mother when he left her side. He learned that behaving as though he needed comfort alleviated her anxiety and so created a false self—a Character—that is needy and anxious. When anxiety is a mother's chronic emotional state, such a child might become conditioned to seeking comfort rather than adventure. Todd developed a Victim Character that drew attention by being incapable. If a child never feels safe, because of mom's constant worry, they will never feel secure enough to explore or learn new abilities that will help them grow to become a healthy adult. This includes being less competent at handling any highly stressful event as they grow to adulthood.[9]

Alternatively, mom might feel better when her child is not demanding attention, when the little one is away from her side—happily exploring or interacting with other children—but may not be able to handle the child's return. For young single mother Jana, it was when little Lissa came back to her for comfort or reassurance that Jana felt anxious and often incapable of supplying her child's needs. She showed this by visibly tensing up when Lissa approached her, by sometimes ignoring her or by distracting her to play away from her mother's side. Even though Jana never physically pushed Lissa away from her, Lissa learned that she was not always welcome back. Because Lissa often had her needs unmet, she learned to behave as though she did not need comfort. With this experience being repeated many times, Lissa developed a Character that was independent and at times quite distant. As she grew she found it difficult to trust people enough to form secure relationships. As a defense against anxiety Lissa had a strong attachment to a locket she never took off, as other children in such relationships might have attachments to objects such as a favorite pencil box, toy, a piece of clothing or jewelry. She would often fall asleep holding the locket in her fist and panicked one day when the chain broke and she thought she'd lost it.

The important thing to realize is that children take their cues about how to behave from their parents. It will not necessarily be from what a parent tells a child or any other verbal communication. Nonverbal communication has far more impact. In particular, the emotional flow that comes through a cord is instantaneous and often indistinguishable from what the child is feeling themselves.

UNRESOLVED PARENTAL ISSUES

When a mother has experienced traumatic events in her past that have not been resolved, especially just before or after the birth of her baby, her trauma can result in some marked behavior patterns in her child.[10] The reason for this is found in the fact that a mother's stress hormones cross the placenta to affect her unborn child and similarly are carried in breast milk. They alter the genetic makeup of the developing embryo and hardwire a child to resonate to the same emotional fluctuations.

The trauma could be the loss of a parent—particularly a mother, or something equally devastating. Over half the parents in one research study had themselves lost a parent through death before completing high school.[11] It makes it hard for such a mother to connect lovingly with the unborn baby within her, or for parents to bond with the baby after birth. The trauma around the death of a parent makes you fearful of losing anyone close to you. To counter this, often the best way through is to consciously let go what you cannot change in the past. Instead, cultivate the present-time relationship you have with your baby, plunge yourself into the unconditional love that is possible there.

CHILDHOOD ABUSE

Abuse might describe parental behavior on a continuum from repeated neglect to severe cruelty that is life threatening. When a parent is not attentive or responsive to their child, or cruel or abusive, a child will inherit much of their emotional style before the child has any choice. Children whose parents are hot and cold, indifferent, overanxious or abusive are prime targets for toxic cords because of the flow of unconscious emotion between their parents and themselves.

In many cases, such as the following story of Peter, a child who has suffered abuse appears apathetic or deliberately aloof when the parent leaves him in a strange situation.

Young Peter was sullen and withdrawn when his father dropped him off and picked him up from school, and unresponsive to most of his teachers. Through early experience he knew that he would not find comfort from his distress with a caregiver. Communicating his needs to his father, an alcoholic, often meant he was punished or simply ignored. Many times he had been left at school when his father had forgotten to pick him up. His mother was the breadwinner and worked long hours at two jobs, leaving her barely enough energy to communicate with her child. The parental relationship was strained and full of resentment, frequently erupting into violence.

Depending on the severity of the neglect or abuse, a child in this situation can develop the chronic tantrum behavior and hostility of Oppositional Defiance Disorder (ODD) or more severe disorders of the Self such as Antisocial or Borderline Personality Disorder. Peter had a collection of army action figures and always carried one in particular with him, a Hell-boy figurine with an enormous gun. As he grew he developed a fascination with guns, missiles and explosives, and at eight was nearly blinded when a homemade rocket he had constructed exploded in his back garden. Before the ambulance arrived, his father yelled at him and gave him a beating for scaring the racing greyhounds he kept in the yard. At school, Peter was caught vandalising a wall with graffiti. A teacher who recognized some artistic merit beneath the obvious antisocial message quietly took Peter aside to discuss art classes, where his talent could develop. He retaliated by vandalizing her car, and she was left bewildered and hurt by the acting out of his hostility—which resulted in a suspension from school and the beginnings of a juvenile criminal record. To Peter, her kindness made him feel weaker, and survival for him meant he had to be tough and suspicious of everyone.

THE LASTING EFFECTS OF ABUSE

When there is an unsuccessful early attachment between mother and infant, it can lead to great difficulty in forming lasting relationships later in life.

In her 30s, Connie had trouble with boundaries and as a result she fears and resents others, including her children, taking over her life, using her time and energy, and generally not allowing her enough space. This shows up in Connie as a disempowered Character—a Victim, Doormat or occasionally a Rebel, among others. When she pushes others away or behaves in a provocative or angry way, she is still reacting to the pressure she feels, due to her lack of boundaries.

Through therapy, Connie is discharging some of her past wounds. She has come to realize she has a choice: that when she feels oppressed in a relationship, to some degree she has unconsciously agreed to it. She is learning to set boundaries, mostly to do with structuring the family's time, that safeguard both her and her children. This takes time and much patience, and she needs self-forgiveness. But the good news is that it is possible to be your own person, to be empowered, to become responsible and to enjoy relationships. Without a parent having done this work, a child can become the target of their rage and resentment, either in willful cruelty or indifferent neglect, or in combinations and variations of these two extremes.

Rowena was an unexpected child. Her older siblings were 10, 13 and 15 when she was born. Her mother was depressed, histrionic and was not aware she was pregnant until she was almost due to give birth. Much of the work Rowena did with me in therapy centered on feeling invisible, unworthy and unappreciated. Not only had her mother not known she was growing within her, but when she found she was to have another child she did her best to miscarry—a tale she often related to the family as though it was amusing. Being unsuccessful in this, it appeared she doubly resented Rowena's existence. Many of Rowena's earliest experiences were of being alone in a crib for hours, crying for someone who never came. As she grew she often remembered being handed off to her siblings for looking after. Her mother was too busy doing other things, caring for the others, particularly her older brother. To compound Rowena's suffering, this brother sexually abused her for a period and when Rowena was 13, on Mother's Day, her mother committed suicide.

Rowena grew up to be a Caretaker Character—loving and overly giving to others, hypercritical and mean to herself. Understandably, Rowena was depressed much of her life. By the time she reached menopause, she felt deep grief that she would never have a child. The relationships she had managed with men were dysfunctional and the longest lasted less than three years. When the formerly abusive brother fell terminally ill, she nursed him, and still managed to make herself feel guilty for not giving enough, before he died.

At this stage, with much therapy, Rowena finally began to give to herself the loving care she had always been denied, and which she had not allowed herself. By caring for herself, she opened to the possibility of a relationship with someone who would reciprocate— someone who didn't use the guilt and manipulative mind games she had experienced with her mother and most of her subsequent relationships.

DETACHING FROM MOM

Detachment between a mother and her child begins when the mother's breast is no longer always or automatically available. Ideally, weaning should be a very gradual process determined by the child in cooperation with their mother, from the baby enjoying their mother's complete attention to increasing gaps in breast-feeding. Through these necessarily small, short disappointments, a child learns to draw on their inner resources to deal with frustration and disappointment later in life. According to pediatrician and psychiatrist Dr. Donald Winnicott, without this process, a child does not learn resilience.[12]

As part of the detachment process, the baby begins to use a comforter, a soft toy, or thumb sucking to represent the comfort and nurturing they experience in breast-feeding. The comforter allows infants to maintain a connection to their mother whenever she is not present and to comfort themselves. This "security blanket" is called a *transitional object* in psychological literature.

At this initial stage of detachment, a "good-enough" parent no longer attends to the baby's every need, and will withdraw from them in gentle, gradual, age-appropriate ways. Problems begin at this stage if the parent continues to be always there, emotionally available and consistently putting the baby's needs first. The child fails to learn to adapt to disappointment or to develop their own resources. They begin to expect that the world will always adapt to them.

Energetically, an infant still exists within the mother's energy field for some time after birth, not seeing themselves as separate. Only the mother's slow withdrawal can foster the growing baby's first steps toward independence, allowing them to exist more and more in their own unique energy field. By the toddler stage, other things being equal, they should be well on their way.

It's not that a toddler with "good-enough mothering" needs their mother less—their mother is still supremely important. The toddler needs her to adjust to their growing independence. They need her to be there, just in case, and they need her to enjoy their explorations and adventures, to make sure they are safe without restricting them, and to welcome them back to her arms.

Eventually though, there is a point at which the cord between mother and child should start to be released, so that the child can begin to be aware of their own emotions as distinct from hers, and so that if the mother has anxiety or other emotions about this phase, they have less impact on the child. It helps enormously if a mother makes the effort to control her nervousness, so her child is not over-whelmed by her emotional baggage. When a mother takes a balanced approach to her emotions, she helps her child handle their own frustrations and anxieties, as much by example as by energetic transfer.

Chapter 6

Mending toxic childhood connections

Like removing weeds in a garden to give space for a prized rose bush to flourish, clearing a cord eliminates what we don't want from a relationship. We clear the rubbish—emotions that belong to another time that are out of place in the present relationship.

Fear of loss makes us either cling to, or ignore, our toxic connections, but the loss we fear is one we have already experienced in our past. When we fear losing something or someone, it is because we are bringing into the present that past loss and pain, allowing the buildup of unhealthy emotions. We can suffocate those we love when we cling. We can also alienate them and confuse them when we push them away so we don't get hurt. We felt it from our parents, our romantic partners feel it from us, and, later, so do our children. Through a cord, we endlessly recycle old pain. Who wouldn't want to be free of that?

When we clear a cord we free that relationship to operate on unconditional love in the present. No longer tied by unspoken expectations, disappointments, blame, shame and hurt, we can relate fully, warmly and openly.

The right time to clear a cord is different for every child and mother. We can recognize this time if either one is watching the other to gauge how to be, instead of interacting spontaneously. I'm not talking about a parent reflecting about how most appropriately to meet a child's needs here: it's when a child holds back from seeking comfort because they feel their mother is uncomfortable with their demands. Or it's when a child's neediness or clinginess is increasingly taking the place of growing independence.

As mothers we may be reluctant to let our child have more freedom, giving ourselves a multitude of reasons why we should remain close. She's too young. He's showing insecurity by crying when I leave him at school. Other children bully him. She isn't making friends. He's more sensitive than the other children.

Through our hormones we are hardwired to care, to show concern, but it is easy to overdo this concern, and end up limiting or suffocating a child.

Our children need our support and a firm structure but not our smothering presence or over-control. We need to step back. While making sure they are in a safe environment, let them fall over and pick themselves up; give a reassuring cuddle if needed. Watch to see if your own neediness or loneliness dictates how close you are to your children or any interaction with them. Alternatively you might feel swamped by their needs and prefer them to not come too close.

Remember that children take their cues from parental behavior and reactions. If a child falls over and we react by rushing over, with distress in our faces and our body language, the child will start to cry regardless of whether they are in pain or not. They can even be conditioned to feel physical pain this way.[13] Keep calm, maintain a reassuring presence. Hug the child without speaking, make sure they are not in danger and then ask, "What happened, sweetheart?" with neutral curiosity. The child will be more likely to respond from their own internal body cues, not from what they think we expect. At the same time, don't show indifference or lack of concern—that will cause your child to pretend to be fine when what they really need is a hug. It can be a razor's edge, at times.

Children who are allowed to make mistakes and learn in a warm, supportive but not restrictive space become independent, resilient, creatively resourceful young people. It's far less likely that a toxic cord will develop between a parent and their child, and all other relationships in the child's life will be healthier as a result.

Believe me, it's worth it.

Increasingly, Generation X and Y remain at home with their parents into their 20s or 30s. Their parents may or may not be happy about it. While there are many logical reasons—mainly financial—for this situation, it establishes a combination of exploitation and need which only further delays a young person's maturity. It prevents them from learning resourcefulness, persistence, patience and tolerance, and it panders to their fear of change. Not a good cocktail for health and well-being.

In this case, clearing a cord between grown children and their parents is an absolute necessity.

Chapter 7

Cutting the cord

A cord that functions well between infants and parents is usually not toxic and therefore doesn't need to be cut. However, as time goes on, a cord can become less nurturing and more intrusive, particularly when there is incomplete differentiation between them. It can be the reason why a developing child grows more rebellious, aggressive or oppositional than is normal, even at certain developmental stages such as the "terrible twos" or puberty. A cord transmits parental expectations and unresolved needs and can stifle a child's emotional, mental and physical development. A child in this situation can believe that they are responsible for keeping one or both of their parents happy. It can prevent the child from maturing into a fully differentiated person. The fact that most of this is unconscious means it cannot immediately be addressed or changed.

There is no hard and fast rule to say when a cord between parent and child should be cleared. In many cases when the child first stamps their feet and says "No!" it is an indication that they need some space and a degree of independence—as well as wise, firm handling.

Cutting a cord doesn't mean complete separation, nor does it mean abandonment. It's about eliminating all the stuff in a relationship that's not helpful—such as blame, holding on to past hurts, unrealistic expectations and disappointments, or projections and emotional manipulation.

Cutting a cord when either the parent or the child is not ready means another cord will form pretty much immediately. It will be less unhealthy than the previous one, at first. It's not long, however, before a new cord becomes full of the same unresolved mucky emotions that neither party wants.

In this case, it's often a good idea to encourage more structured activities outside the home that allow the child some freedom and distance from parental influence—perhaps a team sport, dance, swimming, art classes or whatever the child might be enthusiastic about.

At a certain stage, when *interdependence* is reached, a cord between parent and child is needed only in an emergency, if then. Interdependence is a stage of maturity where we can be independent and at the same time reciprocate in a loving, trusting relationship. For some children, the beginnings of this can be seen at around 12 years of age and increases until they reach adulthood.

Chapter 8

Exploration

In the work I do with clients, clearing a cord is not a matter of simply imagining a gigantic pair of scissors, cutting the imaginary cord and miraculously being free thereafter. While this may work for some, in my experience such purely mental processes are rarely effective. Instead, my client and I enter a gentle period of exploration lasting around two weeks, where, after the initial discovery session, they become aware of every aspect of the dynamics of the dysfunctional relationship. This is far more respectful of the original purpose a cord served and of its influence over the years it has existed. The exploration looks at physical manifestations such as sensations and pain, emotional dumping or draining, other relationships affected and limitations on the person's life.

TOXIC AMALGAM

Susan first came to see me about a vitriolic relationship with her mother, Beth. In session, she entered a space of deep perception, where she saw a cord that flowed to her mouth from her mother's hands. Having encountered cords of this kind where there has been physical abuse, I expected something of this sort in this case. But Susan surprised me. Her mother was a dentist and had treated her own children from an early age. Susan had many painful and unpleasant memories of her mother working on her teeth all through her growing up.

Susan then began telling me about her dreams of drowning in a heavy, liquid, silvery metal that she identified as mercury, or quicksilver. We explored the symbolism of these dreams. In Greek mythology, Mercury was the messenger of the gods who traveled between heaven, earth and the underworld. Susan felt the dreams were about communication and readily identified her need to speak up for herself more, to express her truth. She also saw a need to develop spiritually, to bring more spiritual values into her life, connecting heaven and earth in herself. An important part of this process was to acknowledge certain shadow sides of her personality—her own personal underworld—from which transformation and transcendence would occur. Further explorations into the symbolism of mercury revealed alchemical meanings. Mercury is seen as a passive element in the ancient art of alchemy. Here, too, Susan could relate to how passive she felt she had been for years. She now yearned for the fluidity that mercury also represents.

Susan had been chronically ill for some years. At the same time as seeing me, she consulted a naturopath who suspected that her ill health might be linked to mercury leakage from her dental amalgam. Stunned at the synchronicity of this, Susan had herself tested for mercury toxicity. Results showed there wasn't too much mercury in her system, but Susan was not surprised. She was convinced her sickness was mainly caused by the energetic cord with her mother, rooted in the amalgam laid into her teeth. She then went to a dentist who specialized in biocompatible treatments. Over a period of months, she had all her mercury amalgam fillings carefully removed and replaced with a less toxic substance.

As each filling was treated, Susan's cord-mapping uncovered woundings or samskaras to do with specific events involving her mother. Susan had always been an anxious child who ground her teeth. At times of stress, her temporal mandibular joint—the hinge of the jawbone—became very tense, creating toothache and inflammation in her jaw. At these times, inevitably, her mother gave her dental treatment. She'd also had several root canals, each one accompanied by criticism at the state of her dental care and how that reflected badly on Beth as a dentist.

It was not surprising that Susan associated stressful times with toothaches, not to mention the supreme discomfort of feeling helpless and exposed in her mother's dentist chair for many hours. She felt her mother's anger and disapproval emanating from inside her own mouth. At this point Susan had a dream that it was her mother who held her submerged, drowning in mercury that seeped into every open orifice, poisoning her.

I wondered whether simply removing the amalgam would be enough to free Susan of this unwanted influence, and so delayed the clearing of her cord for a few weeks after her last treatment. It was delayed still further while she had three extractions of old, infected root canals that her mother had done a decade before.

When her jaw had recovered from the surgery, Susan said she felt much better, but she could still feel the cord transmitting a constant stream of criticism and disappointment. It wasn't until after I'd finally cleared the cord that Susan felt free of her mother's toxic influence. At this point, her health began to make significant improvements. A few months later, we discovered and cleared a second cord to her mother, more deeply attached than the first we had cleared. At every stage, Susan felt freer and more herself.

A TOY WITH A LEGACY

The day after Talia moved to a new house, 20-month-old Matti was playing in the driveway next to his mother while she talked to a neighbor. He suddenly let out a sustained wail and Talia looked to see what was the matter.

Matti was red-faced with the serious tears of a very upset little boy. Next to him in the grass was a badly worn little toy dog. Its fur was almost rubbed off. It had stiff, rusted mechanical legs and no batteries. As Talia picked it up and dusted it off, she realized that Matti had picked up the strong emotions she could also feel emanating from the toy.

At the time, I was Talia's housemate. As a trained entity clearer, I tuned in to the toy before performing a clearing ritual on it. It gave a clear impression of a distressed, abused child who had poured all her love and despair into her beloved toy. After the clearing, Matti had no reaction whatsoever to the little toy dog. He simply ignored it, happily chirruping about something else.

Meanwhile, Talia and I wondered grimly about the poor child

whose precious toy had been left behind in the driveway when her family had moved out.

ANXIETY ATTACKS

Not all anxiety results from trauma in childhood, but in the following story it did, even though the original incident had been completely forgotten.

Since he was a small child, William had suffered from agoraphobia. Now in his mid 30s, whenever he was in public spaces, traveling or in unfamiliar environments, his anxiety could be so intense he'd have debilitating panic attacks.

In the safety of the Inner Space technique, a form of relaxed, meditative practice, he described feeling tiny, contracted into a minute space within himself just under his sternum. At times, William even felt dissociated from his body and emotions. As he talked about this experience, I could see William was largely outside his body, squeezed out of his belly and heart, and that he lived mostly in a chaotic, amorphous cloud just above his head.

In his life, in terms of his personal space, William was barely present in his body. He had marked feelings of shame and inadequacy, particularly to do with sex and his sexual identity. He had long suspected some kind of sexual abuse in his early childhood, but had no clear memory of it. In this session I gently brought his awareness down to his belly, encouraging him to keep his focus there as much as he could just by *intention*, with no effort.

After some minutes, William began to access flashes of himself at a municipal swimming pool at around the age of six. He could smell damp air, wet concrete and chlorine, the smell particular to public swimming pool changing rooms and showers/toilets. He began to shiver as the memories acted on his nervous system. He saw himself at the urinals with an older male beside him, a stranger, who scorned his little penis and his attempts to pee. William was paralyzed with fright and shame. He then felt one of the man's hands grab his right shoulder and the other roughly pull down his swimsuit. Then the man anally assaulted William with his finger. As he reexperienced this in the session, William's tension increased and he felt burning around his anus and in his lower back. I encouraged William simply to feel the experience without resistance so it could discharge. His tense body and wrought face relaxed. The burning gradually eased. As his conscious mind accessed and integrated what had happened, the trauma discharged.

William's story continued to unfold. When he went back to his parents at the poolside, he was too ashamed to tell them about the man. He had pleaded to go to the toilet by himself as a "big boy," and wanted to protect what dignity he could. But the shock of this assault had remained with him, buried deep in his subconscious, remaining unresolved till now. It manifested in his constantly feeling small, in his confusion over his sexuality and in his agoraphobia.

I encouraged William to stay with the emotions he had felt in the original incident, allowing himself to feel them more deeply than his child's instinctively protective consciousness had allowed him to remember. As an adult, he realized he now had a greater capacity to handle the assault. He had more and better resources, compassion, wisdom and perspective. And, most important, he knew he had survived this trauma. Within his heart, William the adult comforted the small boy he had been, holding and soothing him, telling him he was safe now; that he, the older William, was there with him and the little boy was not alone. In my session room, William began to feel the constricted space within him expanding. He breathed deeply, more relaxed than he had felt for some time.

When he was calm, the child within feeling safe, William commented that there was an intense sensation on his right hip. Focusing more closely, he described it as an enormous, sucking, tick-like creature with a proboscis and long legs that grasped him around his sacrum, anus, hips and right shoulder. It had a tail, he saw, which connected him to his abuser. Even now, nearly 30 years after the assault, the abuser was sucking William's energy, feeding on his fear and panic. The abuser was not only draining his energy, he was dumping the poison of his own punitive self-disgust, guilt and hatred into William via the cord. William felt the tick-like insect's satisfaction whenever he felt small and confused, or was in the grip of agoraphobia.

After spending a week observing these dynamics, William was able to distinguish between his own energy and the abuser's within the cord that lay between them. Then we cleared the cord. William was relieved to discover that most of the guilt and self-hatred he had felt for much of his life belonged, in fact, to his abuser. What was left—his own residual insecurity and uncertainty—he knew he could deal with. For years he had felt cut off from his lower abdomen, his sexuality, power of will and creativity. Now he felt more present and grounded in his belly. Following up two weeks later, William reported feeling far more like himself. For the first time, along with his new self-acceptance, he felt able to expand his personal space instead of chronically feeling constricted. As he practiced this expansion, his agoraphobia gradually decreased. Two years after this clearing, he had few problems with the agoraphobia that once so limited him.

Chapter 9

Forever baby

The distant past can impact on our lives in all kinds of ways. Danielle's only baby had been stillborn, tragically strangled by the umbilical cord *in utero*. Her deep grief persisted and eventually her husband left, unable to bear it any longer. Many years later she came to see me for persistent depression. I felt the leaden energy in her pelvis immediately, and was not surprised to hear her health challenges included fibroids, cramps, difficult premenstrual syndrome and lengthy, painful periods.

In session, Danielle told me she felt the baby's spirit was still within her. Moreover, she had vowed to keep it safe there, she said. For Danielle, it was partly a desperate fantasy based on her wish to have prevented the baby's death and partly a refusal to let it go. She veered wildly between believing she had "strangled" her son and a total denial of her baby's death. She had refused medical attention after the birth, when the midwife had told her that the placenta had not been fully expelled.

Though Danielle was still unwilling to let go, she agreed to explore the painful heavy energy in her lower abdomen in the hope of relieving her suffering. What we discovered was far from the limpid presence of a baby, or a tiny, lovable infant forever safe under her protection.

Unprompted, Danielle was shocked to uncover an etheric parasite in her pelvis that drained her energy like a leech and preferred her to feel sad and hopeless. It also made her crave and consume fatty comfort foods high in sugar, carbohydrates and salt, which in turn depleted her energy and flattened her mood.

It was still difficult for Danielle to reconcile what she had just experienced with the lovely caring fantasy she had created. It was even more difficult for her to bring herself to let the parasitic energy go, since it meant changing her constant maternal idea of holding her baby safe. Eventually, she realized it was not her baby she was nurturing but her own need for comfort. Once the cord was cleared, Danielle's gynecological problems began to clear up and she was also able to deal with her depression more effectively.

Just as a stillborn baby leaves an etheric residue within the mother's energy field, so does a miscarried pregnancy or an abortion. In most cases this needs to be cleared before a healthy pregnancy can come about. Married for 14 years, 35-year-old Mel was trying to conceive a baby but none of her pregnancies had stuck. Each miscarriage was traumatic, sad and bewildering, as there appeared to be no medical reason she was miscarrying. After she had been working with me for a while, Mel revealed that she'd had an abortion when she was 16, and secretly felt her current inability to carry to full term was because she was being punished by God for having ended her unborn child's life.

In session, when I asked Mel to think of her first pregnancy, she described what she felt as a heavy stone in her heart. It was linked to a feeling of deadness in her uterus with a fear that she could create only dead babies—words that repeated themselves endlessly in her head. Over a period of months we cleared the etheric remnants of each of her miscarriages chronologically in reverse and with each clearing Mel reported feeling lighter and happier. When we came to the abortion, the toxic sludge lining her pelvis was very clear to her as a foreign energy, and not a baby, that drained her life force and her creativity and prevented other embryos from growing to term. It fed on Mel's guilt and grief. Clearing the cord to her dead infant allowed Mel to forgive herself for the early choice she had made to abort her child. At this point, Mel decided it was time to clear a toxic cord to her mother as well, who shared a similar gynecological history of many miscarriages.

A few months later, Mel conceived again. This time she carried to full term and had a healthy baby girl. Mel said she felt able to start afresh, having cleared her sad past away.

After the birth of her baby, Mel realized that she'd had the same number of pregnancies, ten, as her mother. Only three of her mother's pregnancies had gone full term, and one baby had died three days after birth. When a radiant Mel was lying in the maternity ward with her new baby girl cradled in her arms and her mother sitting beside her, Mel confessed to her mother she'd thought she could make only dead babies. Her mother stared at her with surprise and said that she herself had feared exactly that with each of her own pregnancies. Later, in session, Mel realized the cord with her mother had carried to her the same limiting belief that had plagued her mother's pregnancies. It had been imprinted on Mel while she was in her mother's womb and illustrates how powerfully our thoughts are transmitted through a cord.

Chapter 10

Why attachments don't go away by themselves

When strangers make strong instant connections on a first meeting—whether based on affinity or antipathy—it might be because the energy we subtly sense reminds us of someone else with whom we might have a cord, whether we are conscious of it or not. The original cord is activated, and we become confused at the intensity of our emotional reaction—apparently to someone we might not know well. Then a new cord forms with exactly the same dynamic as an old, perhaps buried one.

If we're aware this is happening, we might be able to use focused observation to differentiate the cord from our own energy. In rare cases, we can sometimes simply let it go with intention. We still need to work more on the original, stickier, cord. Generally, the older a cord, the more obscure it is and the more difficult in the beginning to distinguish what is cord energy from our own energy. This older cord may be so entrenched and so entangled with our energy that we need a formal clearing process and ritual performed by a trained clearer.

THE NOT-QUITE-EMPTY
NEST/PARENTAL STORAGE UNIT

When grown up children leave home, leaving their belongings in their parents' home, it's likely neither party is aware to what extent they are maintaining energetic ties. If the cords are not toxic, this may not be a problem. If they are, a spare room stacked to the rafters with old furniture, books, toys and clothes belonging to grown-and-flown offspring can be a festering reinforcement for an unhelpful cord. Unconsciously, some parents hold on to their children by remembering how they were when they were young. This thought carries a definite energy with it that may prevent adult children from fully growing up. The other side of the coin is that grown children's old belongings literally take up space—both physically and emotionally—that could be used for something more vital and healthy in the parents' lives.

For the grown child who has moved out, it's easy to forget they are still responsible for their belongings, obligingly kept by mom and dad. Whether they are aware of it or not, these possessions can hamper their freedom. They've not yet closed the chapter on their childhood.

HOW CAN PARENTS REPLACE A
TOXIC CORD WITH A HEALTHY ONE?

Basia was afraid to cut the cord with her teenage son because of his seemingly thoughtless, risky behavior. She believed the cord was somehow keeping him safe. In fact, feeling Basia's anxiety through the cord spurred her son on to more dangerous activities both to anger his mother and to feel freer. He thought that if he proved to her that her anxiety only made him push the boundaries even further, she would somehow stop being anxious.

After the cord was cleared, Basia was astonished to find that she was less anxious about her son, but also that he was somehow calmer and less interested in taking risks.

Many years later he was in a motorcycle accident and lay injured and unconscious by the side of the freeway. Basia instantly knew something had happened. She had no idea where he was, but calmed herself in order to send him emotionally reassuring thoughts. She began to call hospitals in a way she had done many times when he was younger, but with little panic, simply to find him as soon as possible. As soon as she heard that he was in the emergency room at a hospital some distance away, she was ready to go. While she was naturally worried, she managed to control her anxiety. It was very different to all the other times in her son's teenage years when he'd ended up in an emergency room: this time she knew it was an accident and not in any way intended to punish her. She also somehow knew he would be all right.

Subtle body awareness exercise 1: Etheric sensing

If you'd like to increase your awareness of subtle energy, here are some easy sensing exercises that will help you.

1. Make sure you will not be disturbed during this exercise. Sit in a quiet spot on your own. Close your eyes and rub your hands together rapidly for about 30 seconds. Separate your hands and turn the palms upward. What do you feel? The vibration, buzz, tingle, pulsing or warmth you feel is awareness of your etheric body. Turn your hands to face each other. Very slowly, bring your hands closer and then further away from each other. See how far away your hands are before you lose the sensation you are feeling in your hands. Repeat the exercise as often as you like.

2. Find a houseplant or plant outside. Rub your hands together as in the previous exercise. Now turn your palms to face the plant at a distance of about a hand span. Slowly move your hands up and down the height of the plant, sensing any differences in energy. If you notice that the soil at the base of the plant is dry, water it and see if you sense any difference in the plant's life force. You could try the same exercise with a tree, particularly a conifer or eucalypt, the resin of which is particularly full of etheric energy. If you happen to have a headache, "giving" it to a conifer or a eucalypt can have wonderful results. Trees actually enjoy our complicated emotional energy, as long as we are not intentionally destructive toward the tree. In return, they give us some of their etheric life force and our headache will go away.

3. The next exercise requires a willing partner with an open mind. Sit opposite the other person, about a yard or an arms-length apart, and close your eyes. Rub your hands as before, turn them palm upward for a few seconds, then turn the palms to face your partner. What do you sense, through the air, about your partner's body? What can they tell you about your energy? What happens if one of you moves away?

4. A variation on the above exercise is for one person to sit still with closed eyes. The other person rubs their hands, and then very slowly moves their hands around the contours of their partner's body at a distance of about a handspan from the skin. What do you sense? Is your partner's energy different at various parts of the body? Are there hot or cold spots? Do some parts draw your hand toward them or do some repel the hand? As a healer, I often find my hand is instinctively drawn to the location on the physical body of a client's samskaric wounds. With your partner's permission, you might place your hand on their back, shoulder or arm, to feel any differences when you actually touch with this highly attuned sensitivity. Is your perception helped when you close your eyes? Give feedback to your partner, but know that what we feel and what they are aware of can be two different things: it doesn't mean one of you is right and the other wrong. You can also try this exercise on a pet. Using etheric sensing on an animal is frequently illuminating, and can let you know if your uncomplaining cat or dog is suffering from pain or ailment.

5. Sit facing your partner about an arms-length away and close your eyes. Extending the same kind of attuned etheric sensing, but this time without using your hands, see if you can feel your partner's presence and their etheric body through the space between you. What do you feel? What can they tell you about your energy? It's often difficult to de-

scribe what you might feel. Some words that may be applicable to sensing etheric energy include warm, heavy, light, cold, dry, drawing in, pushing out, prickly, painful, enveloping, soft, smooth, small, constricted, tight, tense, solid, overpowering, strong, gentle, vibrating, pulsing, flat, uneven, vibrant, full or empty. If, however, you start feeling some emotion or other, you are feeling their astral body, which is often mixed in with the etheric. See the next exercise, on page 150.

Part two

Adult Relationships: Up Close and Personal

WHAT are the myths of romance, which, if we believe them, might lead us to devastating disappointment? Why is "chemistry" so compelling, and what is the truth beneath love at first sight? Is it possible to have real magic and passionate connection as well as profound acceptance and unconditional love in our relationships—without romantic delusions?

Chapter 11

The thing about attraction

In the natural course of events, energy is constantly emitted from, and transmitted between, living things.[14] That's why we feel attracted to some people and repulsed by others. We might feel this energy as fleeting, tangible sensations—tingles of excitement or tremors of fear—or just emotions. We will react to these sensations depending on whether we have experienced this energy before, with either a pleasant or unpleasant association. It's the significance we put on that association that activates our energy bodies—the astral/ etheric bodies—in a more lasting way. Similar to electricity that sparks from one terminal to another, there is a strong current between astral bodies. This can then intermingle with the etheric body into—among other things—a cord. In the language of romance, this is often called "chemistry."

When we have an irresistible attraction to someone is it Destiny or have we found our Soul Mate? What about when synchronicity appears to be at work, and we repeatedly bump into someone we are attracted to, in different locations? In most cases, the chemistry we feel is a result of the compulsive magnetism of the scar of an old wound, a samskara. Through our wounds or samskaras, we are attracted to the familiar energy of a situation we've previously known and valued. This might mean we are drawn to a friendship or love even if it is conditional, hurtful, needy or controlling.

Equally we might instantly loathe someone we've never met before because their energy is similar to one that we feared or disliked in the past. If we have not resolved this issue, it will trigger a resonance in our astral-etheric body.

Some believe that when we experience a sudden mysterious chemistry with someone, it will be good for us—a love that is meant to be. Certainly it will be instructive, but not necessarily what we expect. That person may already be in a loving, committed relationship, be gay or just not feel the same way we do. There is more going on than a love indicator here.

So, what's the best response? Firstly, we should not put too much significance on our reactions and attractions. With some introspection we might recognize that we have fallen in love with someone who has our father's hands, the same shaped face as our mother, or the kindness of our grandmother or an old teacher. Separate those attractive elements from the person in front of us and we might see it's a fantasy, as illusory as hanging the clothes of Prince or Princess Charming on a frog. We can become aware of what has stimulated our intense feelings and get perspective.

Energy exchange is a normal part of living and it's one of the great gifts of being human, to share space with another person in a flow of energy. We can often sense/feel another's energy field. Some people's energy is light or warm. Others are tense or have a heaviness about them. An ill person's energy is depleted and feels empty or flat, while a child's is normally free flowing and full of life. Some people's energy is pushy, prickly or angry; some feel jumpy or nervous, forceful or rejecting, or sexually charged. Some seem dangerous and erratic, others loving and accepting. Mostly, we're picking up how they feel about themselves. At the same time we can often sense how they feel about us. And if we have no idea how they are feeling, it may be that we are too self-conscious, with our awareness directed inward more than is needed. It is healthier to allow a free flow between ourselves and the other person.

Some people's interactions are more invasive. These relationships attach themselves to us as cords.

NO WAY IS MY RELATIONSHIP WITH
MY BOYFRIEND LIKE THE ONE WITH MY MOTHER!

Kylie was interested to hear in a lecture that toxic cord relationships with our parents can contaminate later partnerships. However, when she looked at her problematic relationship with her current boyfriend she recoiled at the thought that her attachment to him had anything to do with the antipathy she felt toward her mother. After some reflection, however, she realized that what she wanted from a romantic connection was the safety and warmth she had needed but never got from her mother as a small child. She knew what safety and warmth felt like from overnight stays with her loving, accepting grandmother. Neither Kylie's mother nor her current boyfriend seemed able to relate to her on that level. It became apparent to her that the cord she had with her boyfriend was made of the same longing for love and connection that she felt in the cord with her mother.

Most cords that form later in life occur through a partner or friend latching onto us at an energetic level, forming a cord of energy much like our umbilical connection to our mother in the womb. Unless we remove them, these cords stay with us. Cords function on etheric (life-force) energy, charged with the emotional content of astrality that flows naturally from one to the other. The more they are based on neediness or Character pairs such as Victim/Rescuer, Bully/Victim or Pleaser/Aloof, the more astral the content and the more toxic they are.

The different flavors to cords often depend on the degree of physical contact in the relationship—even if that contact is a thing of the past. A cord with a parent, our children or an old lover can be just as potent as with a current lover, though they will feel different. We may feel tangible physical sensations such as tingles, temperature changes, dizziness or tremors when we think of them—or when they think about us. If they have more etheric content, we can feel energized or drained as though our life force fluctuates around them.

We might have a cord with someone with whom we share a workspace or social interactions but no intimate physical contact. We tend to feel this on an emotional level that can be surprisingly intense and toxic.

When a relationship ends, either through separation or loss, such as death, at first we feel the more physical elements of the cord. In the beginning we can be so devastated all we want to do is sleep or cry or hide away from others, but this eventually will pass and we feel the physical loss less over time. The more emotional elements of the lost connection, however, are not so easily laid to rest.

This is when our mood suddenly changes at the sight of someone similar to our beloved, at the sound of their name or on seeing their photograph. The cord pulls at us, urging us to reestablish a connection based on familiarity, even when the relationship was unhealthy or we have not seen the other for months or even years, or they have died. And unless we have cleared the cord from our previous relationship, it will continue to poison future connections.

ENERGETIC VAMPIRES

Some people feed on others' energy. We can tell when we feel drained after being in their company. Or we can feel "dumped on" by their emotional runoff when they vent anger or frustration. We can feel overwhelmed and become ill when we absorb someone else's anxiety or hostility. This can occur randomly, without a cord, of course. However, if we are frequently in the company of an energy vampire or dumper, a cord usually forms to make it easier for them to feed off our energy.

We can unconsciously form a cord connection if we feel compelled to help someone who doesn't seem ever to become independent of our help. While having a benign or loving intention, we might mistakenly end up being drained, since failure often makes us try harder, often in vain. It's helpful to know that these kinds of cords thrive on repeated interactions and proximity. The other person draws on it, and it usually doesn't help either of us.

If we suspect this is happening to us, it helps to realize that some unconscious part of us has agreed to this scenario. Once we become aware of it and decide it's not in our best interests, we can change it. Often we can do this simply by choosing to detach from the interchange. This means observing exactly how the energetic vampire provokes us, then feeds on our energy. It's the same process when we allow others to "dump" on us.

Abigail's coworker Brenda was an Energetic Vampire. After some time with Brenda, Abigail felt helpless, annoyed and drained. She had no idea what was going on until she stepped back enough to observe every interaction. Brenda would have a problem with her computer, or whatever, and ask Abigail for help. They were small things, but every time Abigail fixed something, something else would go wrong. Abigail found herself becoming more and more frustrated—not with Brenda, but with the computer or whatever had gone wrong. The day Abigail became aware of this process, she caught Brenda looking smug while Abigail felt totally frustrated. All it required for Brenda to stop draining Abigail was for Abigail to say no when Brenda asked for her help. Abigail liked helping people, so this was a challenge for her. She felt guilty at first, but remembering how manipulative Brenda was made her stronger.

It took some persistent practice in refusing. Abigail then watched Brenda turn to someone else for help. It was quite a revelation to observe how Brenda went about the office making others frustrated or angry, and then feeding on that anger. After being a chronic vampire victim, Abigail can now perform her work with her energy intact. She's still happy to help others when there is some reciprocation. She's learned to tell the difference between an energy vampire and someone who can both give and take.

Chapter 12

When old wounds come back to bite us

Maura was the first and only child of 39-year-old Sylvana. The pregnancy was problematic and Sylvana spent most of it lying in a hospital bed, worrying that she would lose her child, sure she would never be able to have another one. When Maura was born the fear and anxiety in which she had been immersed for nine months was evident in chronic nervous clinginess, colic and frequent crying. Her mother would soothe her by playing music, upon which the baby would instantly calm down, listening intently. As a young child, Maura was encouraged to go outdoors, ride her pony, climb trees and swim. Being constantly active kept her from becoming anxious. Sylvana was pleased. It meant Maura was not demanding her attention or getting underfoot in her spotlessly clean house.

A highly intelligent child, Maura did well at school, and with her graceful, willowy body, excelled at dance. Her mother praised her for every achievement, urging her to win and outshine all her classmates. Rarely was Maura praised simply for being herself. Soon

Maura identified herself as a Performer Character who could behave in whatever way got approval. Her first major life-changing decision was to pick dance as a career instead of computer science. She gained scholarships and studied under noted choreographers, developing her skills. Passionate and vivacious, Maura was highly popular and at 23 succumbed to the adoration of Tim, an acclaimed choreographer and teacher who was 10 years older, and married him.

Both Tim and Maura were constantly busy. Dance engagements, seasonal shows, rehearsals and teaching meant that their first passionate year together dwindled by their sixth year into the complacent cohabitation of two acquaintances who spent barely any time together and took each other for granted. When they were in the same place at the same time, their communication was about practical things. They related about nothing deeply emotional, nothing to stir the superficial normality of their lives. Their relationship was stagnating. Each of them was finding stimulation and enjoyment elsewhere.

Tim's choreographic engagements frequently took him out of town, though he maintained the habit of calling Maura before bedtime, just to keep in touch. One night there was no call. Maura was still awake and increasingly unsettled at 3:00 a.m. She grew feverish with worry—not that something terrible had happened to him, but that he was with someone else. She couldn't bring herself to call him, fearing he would be angry. Until this moment, she had never suspected she felt this way.

Maura had a lightning-fast realization that she had always been the more attentive partner. Without examining this threatening thought, Maura retreated immediately into a decision that she no longer cared what Tim was doing. When he returned, neither of them referred to his omitted call. Maura pretended she hadn't noticed.

It took a couple of months for Tim to realize that Maura had stopped putting any effort into the relationship. He grew worried enough to double his efforts, bringing her flowers and gifts, making special romantic dinners. On one such occasion, when Tim had gone to a lot of trouble to prepare a special meal as a surprise, she didn't come home until after midnight. Her rehearsal had gone overtime and she simply hadn't thought to call Tim to let him know. In the ruins of burned-down candles and the overcooked meal, they both half-consciously realized that the Pursuer/Pursued Game they had played had now reversed. That night, what could have been resolved by bringing fears and worries into the open, was ignored, denied and suppressed. The tension between them grew.

Maura was content to be chased but did nothing to deepen the waning intimacy between them. Instead, she formed close friendships with gay men and girlfriends, increasingly shutting Tim out of her life. When these friends formed romantic relationships of their own that took all their time and attention, Maura felt rejected and alone in a way she did not remember feeling before. By now, she had no idea whether she still wanted a relationship with Tim. All she knew was that she was miserable.

When Maura began working on what was making her so unhappy, the sound of her husband's name made her heart race—not with excitement, but with fear. It took some time to uncover what was going on, because Maura's habit was to avoid knowing anything that might make her uncomfortable or anxious, and to distract herself by putting all her attention into rehearsing and performing for others' entertainment. She had no clue about what Tim was feeling. So successful had she been at suppressing her emotions, she barely recognized what they were.

It took great courage for Maura to begin a lengthy period of self-observation. She worked on developing her awareness through listening to what was going on inside her. This meant not resisting the alarming surges of emotion she felt. Over time she began to be able simply to stay with whatever emotion she was feeling instead of pushing it down or rushing to find a diversion. As she did this, after her initial discomfort, the emotion itself became less alarming. She began to understand her own emotions better and this helped her feel more in control of her life.

Maura came to see that what she felt when she tuned in to Tim was his fear of losing her. What she could tangibly feel was a cord filled with Tim's fear. In her inner eye it looked like a thin flexible hose with tentacles encircling her heart. The emotion within the cord sparked her own anxiety and amplified it so she could no longer ignore it or suppress it. She could clearly see the dynamic where each feared the other would find them inadequate and leave.

Maura now knew that beyond her attraction to Tim's dazzling choreographic skill, fame and status, she had been unconsciously drawn to him because they were both emotionally needy. Each believed deep down that they were not good enough, so they defended this vulnerability by pretending not to need love and attention. Both Maura and Tim had experienced similar parenting: their parents were anxious and would also impatiently reject them when overwhelmed by their children's clinginess. In both of their childhoods, performance and achievement was what mattered. Each of them knew what to do, but not how to be. This would have continued, except that Maura's unhappiness forced her to look deeper and see how she really needed to be for herself.

While observing her cord with Tim, Maura realized that whenever she thought of her mother, she felt a flash of anxiety in her chest. Underneath that, she could feel several strands of fleshy, snaky, umbilical-like cords that went from her mother's chest to her own and entangled her. Maura described her end of the cord like tree roots that covered her lungs, heart and stomach, imprisoning her in behavior that was all about trying to keep her mother happy.

In my experience, a more recent cord is generally thinner than one formed at birth or in the womb. The later one often forms on top of an existing cord, is fed by it and feeds it. They share the same emotional charge and can create confusion about whose emotions we are feeling.

Taking time out to observe our interactions is essential before clearing cords. We need to sort out what we are feeling as opposed to what the other person is feeling; and how we react when we feel their emotions dumping on us or draining us. We also need to uncover the original cord on which all the angst of the more recent connection has been built. It's the earliest cord that has set up all the subsequent ones. Below these cords is the original wounding or samskara which then attracts cords to this weakened part of the energy field. In this case, Maura's samskara was her insecure attachment with her mother as an infant.

Maura and Tim are still working on their relationship and on developing a more giving and less needy partnership. It's been a conscious battle to avoid old patterns and to make time for each other and for honest, heartfelt communication. Old habits die less hard when we have a strong motivation to create something better for ourselves and each other, and to see that it is working. Maura continues to work on herself in deepening self-esteem based on who she is rather than on what she can do to impress others. The anxiety that was a legacy of her cord with her mother, now cleared, has reduced to the point that she rarely feels anxious and, when she does, she can consciously calm herself down very quickly.

Chapter 13

Pulling at the heartstrings

Elizabeth felt a pain in her heart when she thought of her father. She had an entirely different sensation when she thought of her mother, however, because that caused an undeniable spasm in her uterus. The toxic cord that formed later in her life to her husband attached to her heart—just like the one with her father. The cord she had with her daughter was connected, as was the one to her mother, to her uterus. Not everyone's cords will follow the same pattern, but there is a general principle illustrated here: we can have several cords attaching to different places on our energy bodies.

In the period of observation before clearing the cord with her father, Elizabeth mapped a samskara that concerned him in her heart. It was from the betrayal and abandonment she felt when he left the family for a lover, early in her childhood. The samskara deep in her belly that underlay her cord with her mother was, naturally enough, about her womanhood and maternal nurturing. Elizabeth was in no doubt that her mother loved her, but also knew her mother had resented having children to support when she was left as a single parent. Blaming men and feeling less independent as a woman was part of it. Both these samskaras created toxic cords in her future relationships.

Cords invariably attach themselves to where trauma has become locked in our body, to an emotional wound or samskara. Basically this wound has breached our energy field. It creates an emptiness of spirit in that spot, from which our consciousness is excluded by buried pain or numbness. The samskara, however, sends out a vibration that attracts a similar energy. As a result of our wounding we're attracted to, or repelled by, the very people whose energy reactivates our old wounds—like Tim did for Maura. Once the cord is formed, it's maintained by the significance we put on the relationship we have with the other person. We may deny this relationship or hate it, resist it or feed it—the end result is the same.

This means that often we are attracted to a romantic partner by our wounds. Their wounds call to ours in empathy and resonance. Relationships formed on this basis offer us the opportunity to heal old hurts, through choosing better, more positive ways of interacting. More often, however, we fall automatically into old patterns of reacting, and fresh wounds restimulate the pain of the old ones.

Very occasionally, there will be two cords—not two levels or variations of the same toxic connection, but a Higher Self connection that might attach between the Third Eye of each partner as well as another cord connecting their wounds. This additional cord means there's an opportunity for these partners to connect on a level of Egoic energy, of unconditional love and acceptance. If either of them cannot rise to this challenge, the relationship will be problematic and toxic, due to the fearful, anxious astral-level connection of their wounds. If, however, they can overcome their fear of rejection or abandonment, their relationship will be a joyous, exciting and fulfilling adventure.

DELIBERATE ATTACHMENTS

While most cords between others and ourselves are created unconsciously, some people set out deliberately to attach themselves to others so they can get what they want.

Dominic was a sharp, intuitive businessman who came to see me because he'd been having dreams that suggested he might have had more than one past life. He found his dreams weird, but so vivid he was curious to explore whether they were symbolic messages of some kind from his unconscious mind or real memories and experiences. Over a series of sessions he uncovered two lives as a Native American shaman, and was humbled and surprised to discover the reverence in which his people had held him, and their respect for his wisdom and vision. He had never known how much others thought of him in that life because his spiritual vocation meant he had kept himself aloof from everyday village life. The message, he believed, was that now his task was to allow someone closer, to find a soul mate to share this life. As sessions proceeded, I noticed something that felt persistently not-quite-right. I asked Dominic if he ever felt emotions or sensations that seemed extreme or out of place, or perhaps a part of his energy that felt foreign.

To my surprise he answered quite matter-of-factly—was I referring to the snake? He coiled his left arm to simulate the raised head of a snake. Intrigued at how closely this corresponded with what I had seen, I asked him to tell me what he had noticed.

In the last few months, he'd felt a creeping sort of warm energy that began in his left big toe and traveled up to his groin, where he felt a burning sensation. It tracked up the center of his body to his heart, where again it burned, but in a coiling constricted kind of way. It snaked out to his left shoulder and to his fingertips. He assured me he wasn't worried about it. He had often noticed weird, transient sensations in his energy field since beginning meditating and working on himself and had assumed this was just another passing phenomenon without any particular significance. I suggested it might be a good thing to investigate this. He was willing, though convinced it meant nothing.

The technique I use at such times takes clients deep into the Third Eye, the organ of subtle perception between the eyebrows. In this inner space of vision, Dominic identified the emotions that accompanied the various sensations he had described to me. Dominic was astonished at the degree of longing and grief he felt. As he put it, it was as if the snake was "strangling my heart." Around his leg and groin he felt something like strands of barbed wire. When I asked him to see where this sense of restriction was coming from, he saw a cord made of barbed wire that came from "somewhere out there, someone I can't see." Once in his body, it took the form of a boa constrictor that coiled sinuously through his body.

I asked Dominic if he had noticed any changes in his life recently that might be connected to these sensations. He replied that, though he'd not noticed a connection before now, he'd had an unusual reluctance to go out on dates lately. It was as though his ability to communicate with women, normally free and unforced, was somehow blocked.

Coming out of the session, Dominic repeated how surprised he was that the "boa constrictor," which he had considered "just energy," was actually affecting his life. He agreed it had all the hall-

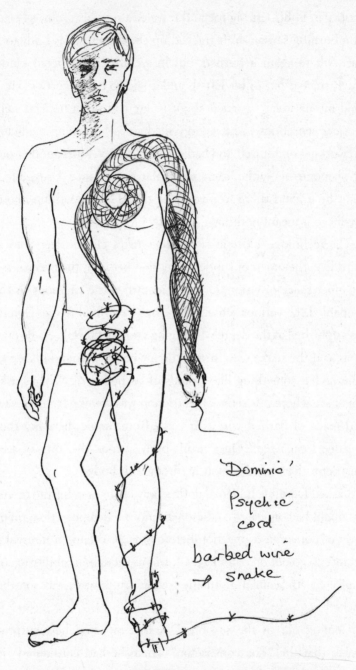

'Dominic'

Psychic
cord

barbed wire
→ snake

Dominic felt the cord started as barbed wire and turned into a snake.

marks of an energetic cord. As is my usual practice, I asked Dominic to draw the cord as he saw and felt it. It's a part of cord exploration that helps objectify the foreign energy to distinguish it from our own feelings and emotions. It also helps detachment—to "get it out," on paper, at least.

After another session of exploration, I cleared the cord. He still had no clue who was on the other end of the cord, though he had remarkable clarity on every other aspect of this phenomenon. I was reminded that this was a man who in previous lives had already developed extraordinary spiritual insight, which made him much more able to read what was going on.

Following the clearing, Dominic's previous easy flow with women returned and he began dating again. A month or two later he found someone special enough to consider a serious relationship. He told me he was happier than he ever remembered. Sessions stopped for a period of time while he gave all his energy to creating the new partnership.

I was soon to hear a harrowing twist to this happy story— something to make me consider cords in a whole new light. About three months after I'd last seen Dominic, a new client, Kathy, came in with a sad tale of unrequited love. The previous year she'd met a gorgeous man who didn't know she existed. No matter how much she tried to get his attention it appeared he wasn't interested. We began exploring the cord connection she felt with him. It was full of painful longing and rejection. Then Kathy quite calmly told me something that made my hair stand on end.

She practiced a form of benign witchcraft, she said. Some eight or nine months ago, longing desperately for this man whom she was convinced was her soul mate, she had made a binding spell. She described a delicate rambling rose. She had imagined sending this rose to climb his left leg and bloom as a red rose in his heart. It was intended to ignite a passionate love in him for her. In daily rituals she had poured all her love and longing into this spell. But it hadn't worked. He still failed to notice her. Sadly, she concluded it was obviously not meant to be. She sighed, using his full name.

It was Dominic.

Client confidentiality is something I take seriously. I couldn't let Kathy know Dominic's side of the binding spell experience, nor that he had been to see me, amazing coincidence as it was. I wondered whether it was the cord between them that had led to them both coming to see the same therapist, unbeknownst to the other. Nothing of this sort had happened in my practice before.

I warned Kathy gently and in a general way that binding spells were more likely to create toxic cords, since they were intended to force what should be natural affection. Having discovered through her own process of cord-mapping how intensely painful the cord actually was, Kathy nodded with greater understanding.

For me it was illuminating to see that no matter how well-intentioned Kathy believed she was, a toxic cord resulted. There is not a great deal of difference, except in intention, between what Kathy had done and a curse, formed of deliberate and conscious ill will directed toward another person in daily rituals. Instead of igniting passion as she intended, she merely transmitted her loneliness and anguish, while rejection and indifference came back to her. So it had the opposite effect than intended. Her actions restricted Dominic's heart and interfered with his social life until the cord was cleared.

Chapter 14

Breaking up

ENDING CYCLES

Like a story with a beginning, middle and end, relationships have phases in a cycle. Whether we're talking about the entire cycle of the partnership or daily cycles that center on our work or activities, each phase has a different feel. But each is essential to the whole cycle, just like a story. Ending one story allows another to begin. Not ending properly means we sometimes can't begin the next story with our full attention. The ancient Hindu concept of the three action cycles in life or *Gunas—rajas*, *satva* and *tamas*—apply excellently to relationships—let's see how.

The rajas phase is the enthusiastic energy of beginnings. Effortless and full of joy, passion and potential, the energy of rajas is that falling-in-love and honeymoon period of any liaison. Obstacles seem to be easily overcome and the future seems bright. Caught up in our desires, there's a marked increase in sexual activity and a general heightening of energy stimulated by the excitement of sexual attraction and pleasure. It is a happy period.

The next phase is satva, the time of fulfillment and having reached a goal. This describes sexual satisfaction, and also relates to the phase of a relationship when maintenance is paramount. We want to keep the good feelings happening in an ongoing way, even if they are not all at the rajas level of high peaks of excitement. Ideally, when a partnership is based on equality, respect and good communication in all areas, this phase can be relatively effortless. We sustain our partner and ourselves through reciprocated attention and loving care. We create a positive future for each other with honest communication and consideration. There are many helpful nuances such as taking care to appreciate our partner, thanking them when appropriate, not taking them for granted, and making agreements only when we know we can keep them, thus avoiding letting our partner down. It entails being in the present with our partner, recognizing when old baggage from past connections comes in to make the time we spend together sour or stale, and choosing better ways of relating. In satva, we are keeping our relationship vital, exciting and nourishing by constant injections of creativity. We are keeping love alive by our awareness of the shared love that surrounds our partner and ourselves.

Tamas is the energy of endings. Like sleep that ends each day, it is a necessary time of recharging. In a relationship, it might mean a time when we are involved with our personal concerns that may not directly include our partner—with work, hobbies, friends, time alone or meditation. Of course these indirectly add to our relationship when, reunited with our partner, we have been enriched and recharged by time apart doing other things.

Tamas also refers to the ending of relationships. Some relationships are not designed to last forever. Sometimes the purpose of the relationship is to enable us to learn something about ourselves, and to grow past our old limitations.

We fear endings because they are like death. The future is unpredictable and change can feel unsafe. We fear leaving our partner alone and not knowing his or her future, we fear hurting the person we have a shared history with, we fear being replaced by someone our partner prefers. It's natural to feel this concern, but if it's too difficult to live together in harmony, then you are just prolonging the agony. The benefit of the time spent together is over, and if the relationship is not ended cleanly and with respect for each person, it becomes very mucky and needlessly painful.

The messiness in breakups comes from not being clear about what you want. If we were clear on this, even the fear of change would not stop us. We can put off ending a relationship because it's more comfortable to stay, even though we are not doing the best for ourselves or our partner. In this case, if we are not actively creating the relationship in satva, the entropic aspect of tamas comes into play and the relationship will dwindle in any case. At this point it's good to ask yourself, can you make your relationship work?

A partnership is about each person pulling the load equally, and together, thus making the experience lighter, or cocreating something joyful that nourishes both of you. If that enthusiasm and sharing has gone, it's time to examine what you need and what you need to do. Have you both tried absolutely everything you can to make it work? If only one of you has tried—you—what does that tell you about your partner's commitment? If your relationship is problematic, consider this. If you were to see your partner walking toward you now, as though for the first time, would you still fall in love? Would you still begin a partnership? If the answer is yes, then there may still be life and purpose in this relationship. If the answer is no, it's time to move on.

Many of us find all kinds of excuses for not doing what we know would be best. We need to be very honest with ourselves. What is the benefit in staying? If you are burying your need to grow and expand for your partner's benefit, consider what you are doing to him or her that equally might be preventing their growth.

If there is no longer any way for us to grow within a partnership, there is a skill in ending it gracefully. Unless fear or anger has made one or both people unreasonable or demanding, it is possible to end a relationship with love. We do not need to end it painfully or angrily. We do not need to vilify our partner or blame them to make it easier to walk away. We do not need to involve lawyers or get into disputes about possessions. If our partnership has been mutually beneficial but is now something we have outgrown—even if it has lasted decades—there is no reason we cannot end it with the same respect and love we have always had, knowing the future will be better for both of us. Despite this, know that endings are usually sad, but sadness passes.

However, if we are separating because we can no longer bear a toxic cord, there is usually more pain and anger than there needs to be. Along with resentment and acrimony, this ends up only making divorce lawyers wealthy.

Fear of endings often relates to our fear of death. If so, we need to be mindful that we are trading off essential aspects of who we are to avoid dealing with this fear. Endings are far easier if we can walk consciously through them, staying alert to all the nuances, including the gifts that are also there. To do this we need to stay in the present, knowing that we must let go of the past in order to move on to something better, to our next cycle, even if that is about learning how to fill our lives with joy and richness alone.

TILL DEATH US DO PART

Marilyn was convinced she should stay in her marriage because she wanted to honor the vow she'd made to love and honor, through sickness and in health, for richer for poorer. Her husband had developed a long, debilitating illness that changed his personality and made him irrational and violent. Marilyn was determined to adapt and cope with the situation. As she usually did, she devoted herself to her husband and children, but took little care of herself, and one day she collapsed in exhaustion. Soon after that she was diagnosed with clinical depression and began taking medication. It enabled her to struggle on, but nothing else changed. In therapy, I asked her what would happen if things went on the way they were. Apathetically, she said she'd probably get so sick she would die. The problem looked too enormous to tackle. Marilyn felt leaving the marriage was simply not an option. After all, it wasn't her husband's fault that he had gotten sick. Who would look after him? Wasn't it her duty?

But it continued to wear her down. Her husband's personality changes meant everyone around him had to accommodate him, pacify him and keep him calm at all costs. Eventually, Marilyn realized that vowing to love and honor her husband forever did not mean her health and well-being were less important than those of her husband or their children. In fact, by wearing herself out the way she was continuing to do, she would soon not be there for them at all.

Marilyn reexamined her priorities. To truly help her husband

and herself, and to be there for her kids, she needed time off and more support, she needed to look after herself. Beginning to put these in place a little at a time, Marilyn was more hopeful, healthier mentally, emotionally and physically, with more energy to do what she believed was the right thing.

There were many turning points for Marilyn in the process of extricating herself from a marriage that had become a cage in which she felt like a whipped dog. One was in realizing the enormity of the problems her husband's illness would create and what that would mean for her and her children's future. For a short time Marilyn slipped into the trap of blaming her husband, to justify leaving him, to make it easier. She soon came to her senses. There was no one to blame. It was no one's fault. Another turning point was in the exploration of her cord to her husband.

In the deep inner space of the session, Marilyn saw two cords between them. One went from her husband's throat to her throat. Its main function was for Marilyn to pour honey on her husband's irrational angry outbursts, to mollify and placate him—ineffective as this was. The other cord branched from his right hand to her heart, where it thickened bulbously, dumping her husband's need to control her and everything around him into Marilyn. Beneath that need to control, she realized, was his fear, and as she allowed herself to feel it, it clutched at her heart. She wondered whether her depression was in part her husband's fear and anxiety, and remembered that the cord had formed before they began their relationship, when he first revealed to her his extreme loneliness. Her heart had ached to help him and she felt her energy reach out and encircle him, to console him and surround him with love. Wryly, Marilyn recognized a Rescuer Character. Much too late to prevent heartache, she now knew that rescuing never boded well for an equally supportive relationship.

In the sacred space of the cord clearing ritual, Marilyn felt the bonds of her equally sacred vow to her husband finally dissolve. She was free, and it felt clean, joyous and optimistic. She looked forward to the future—which would not be without its challenges—without the murky confusion of her entangled marriage.

Chapter 15

What happens to connections when we die?

In a hospital room late one night, two middle-aged daughters and their husbands are gathered quietly around the bed of Bill, 89, dying of coronary heart disease. Everything that can be done for his comfort is being done. Bill's family have been here at his bedside for a week, and are as prepared as they can be. They have agreed with Bill's request that "no heroic measures" be taken to resuscitate him. None of them is afraid of death. They see it as a part of life and, privately, each of them has already released any ties they feel to him. They have told Bill it is okay with them for him to go. They have all said good-bye. And yet, it seems Bill's body is not quite ready to shut down completely. The process seems slow for all of them but they are patient for the time to be right for him.

Bill lies with eyes slightly open but it seems he is not seeing what is in the room. His breathing is rough and irregular in a kind of hitching gasp between increasing phases of no breath at all. It is a little distressing to the family. Earlier, a nurse told them this was called Cheyne Stoke breathing, quite normal at this stage, and added a pillow behind him so he could breathe more easily.

Now, Bill's face grows suddenly animated and his stare focuses on a point a few feet in front of his face. He makes an effort to sit forward and raises his right hand as though in greeting, or to touch someone only he can see. Whoever it is, the sight softens his face in a delighted smile. Though he tries to speak, just a croak emerges and he falls back exhausted onto the pillow. His eyes close a fraction more. He takes another gasping Cheyne Stoke breath.

His family look at one another, tears starting in their eyes. One of the daughters takes her father's hand and quietly remarks to the others how cold he is, though the room is warm. The other daughter stands and strokes her father's face. The room is full of love. They are all at peace with what is happening.

Knowing that the sense of hearing is the last to go in the dying, one of the sons-in-law suggests they sing to Bill, and they start quietly with songs they know he loves. At 4:00 a.m. when a nurse pops her head in the door to check that all is okay, Bill's condition has not changed.

Two nurses arrive to turn the patient and take vitals and the family troops out. When they return Bill is at last silent and still. It is obvious he has gone. What made him the person he was is no longer there.

It is common in the dying process for the dying person's etheric body to drain life force from anyone in the vicinity and even from fresh flowers in the room. There doesn't need to be a toxic cord for this to happen. By its nature the etheric body grasps after life, and even the flowers in the room are now withering. In Bill's case, there is no toxic cord between him and his family. They are holding him energetically in his dying process, but not holding on in any way. Nevertheless, it was when Bill was left alone briefly that his etheric body could no longer find life force in the environment, and could finally let go.

After a little while one of the sisters sets up the clearing ritual they have previously agreed to. It is obvious to her that the spirit has left the body. She sees that the etheric body also has left the physical body and is already fragmenting, returning to the etheric pool. Using higher consciousness, she closes her eyes, checks in the astral space where Bill is, and finds him going through his life review. As sole judge of how well he achieved his life's task, Bill is viewing his entire life in flashes that go more quickly than physical time would allow. He sees it all, understanding without regret what he has missed, accepting his triumphs and failures with equanimity, seeing his next life and what his task will be. Waiting solemnly on either side of this soul in transition are the two enormous Sentinels of the land of the dead. Their presence ensures that only truth will do here. Self-delusion and self-justification fall like ash. It is a cleansing of the soul before returning to the oversoul, the true Self. Also in this space are those whom Bill loves who transitioned before him, his wife among them. It is a gentle, joyful welcome, and they sustain and hold him gently through the next stage.

As his daughter begins the chanting of the clearing ritual around his physical shell, Bill is undergoing the phase of shedding his astral body. Letting go of his earthly identity, his history, his achievements and his attachments, will allow him the much deeper and complete connectedness of spirit. It's not difficult for him. He has been ready to end his earthly life for some time.

The chanting takes around 15 minutes. The clearing deals safely with all the astral and etheric fragments from Bill's body, fallout that might otherwise land on those in the vicinity. Afterward, feeling the relief that comes when a loved one's suffering is over, the family leaves. In a mood of celebration at the life of their father, they decide to take a walk in the park near the hospital in the dawn mist together.

As they walk past the nurse's station, they stop to thank the staff for all their help. They cannot help but notice the weeping woman leaning against a wall outside another private room. The woman, whose name is Anna, has been here for a few days. Her mother is dying of cancer. One of Bill's daughters has spoken to her before and goes up to exchange a word or two. Anna told her previously that she has been looking after her mother on her own long before the end stages of her cancer. She never married and now she feels it's too late. Bill's daughter touches Anna compassionately on the upper arm. Anna nods with eyes downcast, and after a little while goes back into the room where her mother lies. Bill's family leave the hospital for the last time.

Anna's mother lies shrunken and yellow, curled up on her side in a fetal position in the middle of the white pillows and hospital sheets, a tube to a urine bag snaking from her to a bag on the side. Her eyes are fixed and glazed, and she, too, has Cheyne Stoke breathing. She cannot move on her own and the nurses must turn her every two hours. There are four family members besides Anna in the room, her two brothers and their wives, and the others don't want to be here. They find it oppressive and morbid. They've been here all night, trying to sleep on hospital armchairs brought in from the visitors' lounge. The younger pair look bored and are thinking of going outside for a smoke. Shortly they do leave with the other sister-in-law, and Anna looks at them reproachfully as they go. Anna's elder brother stays out of guilt, but wonders privately how long this will take. He asks Anna if she wants breakfast and she shakes her head. He mutters something about the coffee machine in the corridor, and leaves.

Anna gazes at her unresponsive mother and starts, haltingly, to speak to her. What pours out of Anna is a litany of regret, self-blame and guilt for the few occasions in the last few years she took time away from looking after her mother, to go to a movie or meet a friend for coffee. Mixed with this is long suppressed anger at being trapped, of not being able to live her own life as she might have, to get married and have children, or to find a career. Anna has never been able to express this to her mother, since she believes she is a bad person even to feel it, so she directs that anger at herself. Long ago her mother used to tell her repeatedly that Anna was selfish and vain, and Anna now carries all that criticism within her. The cord between them is thick and suffocating, but neither could do without it because they believe it means love and care. However, along it comes all Anna's suppressed anger and resentment. It poisons both of them.

Now, Anna is becoming hysterical, choking on sobs as she begs her mother to forgive her and not to die, not to leave her. Eventually she stops crying, and after looking at the wooden, glazed look on her mother's face for a long moment, goes into the bathroom for a drink of water and to wash her face. While she's in there, her mother's Cheyne Stoke breathing finally stops. When Anna comes back to her bedside, her mother is dead. Anna's brother comes back into the room, sees his sister crying "Mamma, Mamma" and clutching at the body, and immediately runs out to find the others.

The spirit of Anna's mother hovers above the body, looking

down in confusion at the grief-stricken Anna, hugging and clasping the empty, shrunken shell on the bed. Soon, the others come in. The astral and etheric fragments should now be set free from the body, but instead, the fragments are attracted, as they were in life, to the cords that joined Anna's mother to her family. Feeding on their etheric life force, and the various emotions of grief, anger, resentment, need and blame, these toxic cords to her family hold back her astral body and prevent it from completing its journey. It will take a great many years before the spirit is released, if ever. Unless Anna's family learn to let go of their mother and all the emotions they feel about her, the cords will continue to tie them together.

Like a burning off of the dross so only pure gold remains, the fragmentation of our astral and etheric bodies at death can be an intense experience in more than one way. Since our astral body is made of samskaras, the grasping nature of this body of accumulated emotional pain is just as difficult to release for the dead as it is for the living.

In truth, these emotions we've been conditioned to feel through past experiences are transitory. If we simply let ourselves feel them, they will pass quickly with no more permanent effect than water through a net. But the more we try to push these sticky energies away, the more they gain energy from our resistance and the more they stick. We can greatly help the inevitable disintegration of our subtle bodies after death by practicing letting go while we're still alive. It's really just about letting go of illusion and our attachment to it.

As different as tin is from gold, the fleeting emotions we are used to suffering in our astral body do not compare with the feelings of the Egoic body and our Higher Self. More a state of being and the natural essence of spirit, the feelings of the Higher Self are sublime states rarely reached in earthly life. The closest that we might feel to them while we are alive are enthusiasm, joy, serenity and unconditional love. When, like our Higher Selves, we feel universally connected to the whole of creation, our former cord connections seem as insubstantial as cobwebs.

SUICIDE

Except in cases of the mentally ill or when a terminal illness with extreme chronic pain leads to voluntary or assisted self-euthanasia, when people commit suicide the ongoing negative significance they've put on events and experiences in their lives is extreme. In most cases it's precisely because they are unable to let go of these negative experiences that they end their lives themselves. It might be an act intended to end unendurable emotional suffering, but unfortunately it has the opposite effect.

Sometimes a person committing suicide is self-absorbed, unable to lift themselves out of this trap and unable to consider the devastating effect of their death on others. Some take their own lives to avoid shame to themselves or their families. Some suicides intend to wreak revenge on the living, to punish or hurt them by their final action. Because of the two-way toxic flow of psychic cords, much of what the person who committed suicide felt while still alive might not even have been their own emotions. This also means that in the period after death, the suicide's realization of the pain caused to loved ones can add to the huge amount of emotion those left behind experience through cords.

SUICIDE CONTAGION AND CLUSTER SUICIDES

Occasionally we hear reports of a cluster of suicides, mostly around teenagers and young adults. They happen when the friends and loved ones of a person who has suicided—and even strangers who happen to live in the same area—feel irrational compulsions to follow suit. Known as suicide contagion, the situation puzzles and distresses social services, often leading to investigations about possible suicide pacts.

Cords give us an interesting explanation for what is going on in these situations. Where there are cords with the deceased person, those left behind get a direct injection of overwhelming pain and hopeless thoughts. Cluster suicides occur mostly in small communities where people have known one another for many years. A suicide attempter may not know the deceased, but when they learn about the death through media reports, it's likely the attempters identify emotionally with the successful suicide in some way. Astral fragments from the deceased person do the rest.

The effect of cluster suicides on a community is so devastating that responsible media outlets will now not publicize the stories. It is very important, therefore, that we know how suicide contagion spreads—and that the feelings of hopelessness or bleakness we might have following the suicide of a friend or acquaintance are probably not all our emotions. Naturally we will feel sad, but sadness passes.

In the normal scheme of things all these intense feelings are transitory, and only if we resist them in some way do they stick. Knowing we are absorbing emotions from the environment and feeling them as though they are ours—though they are not—hopefully means we can step back, and let them go.

CLEARING THE CORD OF A SUICIDE

In my book *Let Your Past Go and Live* I told the story of Teri, who, despite an enthusiastic love of life, suffered from episodes of depression and had a Suicidal Character.[15] Teri had a strong cord with her mother, Lynn, who also suffered from severe depression. Despite her best efforts Lynn was unable to give her daughter the affection she needed. Lynn had attempted suicide many times and avoided all treatment. Her death wish was not just the deeply seated melodrama of a Character: life was hell for Lynn and she simply wished to avoid it.

The sudden, unexplained death of Teri's older sister Mandy awoke in Lynn samskaric echoes of Lynn's father's suicide when she was pregnant with Teri. On the anniversary of her older daughter's death, the still unresolved emotions in her cords to her deceased father and daughter were amplified to the point that Lynn finally succeeded in ending her life.

Lynn's depressed emotions had long fed Teri's Suicidal Character while she was still alive, but when she suicided, the cord between her and Teri was filled with despair and her intention to end her life. Because cords are made of astral substance, all emotions within them are intensified and magnified. These emotions and thoughts landed in Teri.

Fortunately Teri was able to find support for this onslaught before doing anything rash. The most important part of Teri's process was in differentiating who she was apart from her mother. It began with sorting out which emotions were hers and which were Lynn's. Where Teri's Suicidal Character's thoughts and emotions were all about getting attention and punishing those she felt were responsible for her pain, her mother's emotions were not involved with blaming anyone else. She simply wanted to end her own emotional pain—for which suicide is not a solution. The cord-clearing that followed eliminated the toxic cord, enabling Teri to take responsibility for her own emotions—which she was able to do with time.

Chapter 16

Letting go

I have worked with clients who believed an energetic cord drew them to be born into the same family twice after they died in childhood or infancy the first time. More common is the belief that people have been reincarnated with the same parents as in a previous life. Quite often, people believe they are currently in a relationship with someone they loved in a previous life. I have never been able to corroborate this, but it's theoretically possible if the cord is extremely strong at death. An example of how it might be possible is given in this next sad story.

In 2006 British newspapers reported the tragic case of a triple suicide in Wales. The 27-year-old only son of a couple in their 50s hanged himself after some months of unemployment and subsequent depression. The next day, the parents made an unsuccessful attempt to gas themselves in a car after swallowing tablets. Shortly afterward the man drove his wife to a reservoir where she was later found drowned. He returned home and hanged himself.

What part might energetic cords have played in this tragedy? It's likely that, like most parents, these folks had at least a certain amount of expectation and disappointment about their 27-year-old unemployed son. They witnessed his depression and no doubt felt helpless. In a cord, these emotions would intensify his self-recriminations and depression, and in a vicious cycle perhaps contributed to his actions.

At the time of his suicide, the parents' anguish at the loss of their son and their resulting sense of futility is sent along the still active cord to the deceased young man. This, and intense regret at what he has done, now combines with his depression and cycles back to his parents through the cord. Then he enters the intense period of the "shedding" after death—when we let go of our earthly life and who we thought we were—so the spirit can move on. At this point, a strong cord can prevent the soul's progress. This, too, goes back along the cord to the parents and their suffering becomes unbearable. It means the parents' suicide may not have been of their own choosing.

With this level of emotional fusion between the son and his parents, as well as unresolved aspects of their relationship, it could theoretically be enough to draw them to reincarnate as a family once again, to face the same issues. Tragically, this area in Wales is currently one where the phenomenon of cluster suicides is a significant problem. This story points most strongly to a need for us all to differentiate from the emotional turmoil of those close to us—not in a callous way, but so we can simply be there for support instead of being overwhelmingly affected. Handling our own sad response, which will pass, is completely different from being merged with the problems of others—which are not ours to solve.

BREAKING THE CYCLE OF ADDICTION

Tony struggled with alcoholism and had been in recovery for over 12 months, attending AA meetings and keeping himself healthy until he lapsed and went on a bender. He had been under a lot of stress, but a combination of sudden unhappy events including a breakup with his girlfriend and being made redundant at his job made him lose the will to implement all his usually helpful strategies. Once he sobered up he determined to fix up his life, starting with clearing a cord to his ex-girlfriend with whom he had had a codependent relationship. Over a number of sessions during which we found and cleared cords and their underlying samskaric wounds, Tony finally uncovered a particularly caustic cord to his deceased father, also an alcoholic. In fact, his father had died of alcoholic poisoning and cirrhosis of the liver. When Tony traced back over his own worst periods with alcohol abuse, he realized it had started around the time of his father's death when he was 22. At that time, he told me, he had long been disgusted at what alcohol did to his father and decided he would never drink himself.

After his father's death, however, he had felt an overwhelming compulsion to drink himself into oblivion every weekend and soon was drunk every night of the week. The cord was still feeding his desire to drink, but Tony now knew it was not his desire but his dead father's. Unable to enjoy the effect of alcohol since he no longer had a body, the entity that had come along the cord from his father would not let him rest until he was dead drunk. The cord was especially desperate for alcohol if he had not had a drink for a few hours and grew stronger when Tony was intoxicated. It fed on his self-pity while it increased his self-loathing and despair.

Clearing this cord was a mammoth undertaking as Tony realized it had controlled him for over 20 years. Through it, Tony felt his father was raging angrily at him as he used to when Tony was a boy; blaming him, hitting him and constantly putting him down. This cord had influenced all his relationships, his jobs and his poor employment record, as well as his health. After the clearing Tony felt he had recovered his young self again. He is especially pleased that he has not had the slightest desire to drink since the clearing, and he has a new romantic relationship based on shared interests, mutual respect and equality rather than dependence. For the first time in a long time, Tony feels optimistic about his future.

ALLOWING GRIEF

If a loved one is near death and there is a risk of astral fragments attaching themselves to us, we can take steps that will free us from harmful attachments, even without a clearing.

If we simply allow our grief to take its natural course, there is less chance of holding the deceased back from their great journey. Not resisting our sadness means it passes as it should, in time. If we resist, suppress or overindulge in grief, we can draw fragments to ourselves and maintain a toxic cord.

One simple outward practice is to wear white at the funeral, as is customary in Hindu and Buddhist ceremonies. Dark colors, especially black, attract heavy energies. While white may seem inappropriate for a funeral in Western cultures, these days the tradition of wearing black is not so strongly kept. Make the funeral and the wake a celebration of the life of your loved one and wear white or some light joyous color. These colors will help repel astral fragments as well. While you miss them, ultimately the funeral is simply the end of a day's traveling. It's nowhere near the end of the journey.

You serve yourself and your loved one best when you let go of the intense emotions you are feeling. If it feels impossible to loosen the grasp of loss and pain, having the intention to let go is a powerful start, even if it feels impossible. Try to allow the emotional waves to flow through you without significance. Don't worry at this stage if it's difficult to discern whether it's your pain or the deceased's. Feel it, honor your loved one fully with complete acceptance, then let the emotion go.

It's important to know that the attachments we are letting go are not to the spirit of our loved one but simply to their earthly shell, their physical body. All being well, their spirit, now freed of matter, has passed over to other realms where we will meet them again.

In many cases, cords between elderly partners who have been together for many decades means that when one dies, the other follows soon after. It may be that without their lifelong companion, life seems to be not worth living. It may be that the connection between them has sustained them both for many years. It may not be a toxic cord that joins them. In some cases, sheer loneliness and a strong cord that holds the deceased back unless the spouse joins them, can be what causes the soon-after death of the survivor.

Some years ago I watched an interview with the bereaved wife of a famous humanitarian whose family had been around his bedside when he died. With tears in her eyes, she described how each family member later shared with the others how they'd felt "little pieces of

Tom" land on them on his passing. The widow felt this was a great gift, that each now had a part of their departed loved one. Much later, I read another interview where she described the burning passion she had received from her late husband to continue his philanthropic work, something she had promised him before his death she would do. While there's no doubt this gracious and energetic woman fully believes in the same causes her husband espoused and has tirelessly increased the scope of his benefactions, it is important to know that we have a choice. There might be some legacies of the deceased we may not wish to be driven to continue in this way, unless we are ourselves dedicated to them.

Like cords to the living, an important part of detachment is to identify what comes from the other person and what is ours. Once we are over our initial grief, we do need to work on ourselves, possibly with the help of professionals, so we can resolve our own emotional baggage. As for the rest, let the flow of emotions go back to the person it belongs to, so they may deal with their issues and their process, even after death.

A LIFELINE

When my father, Alan, was 86, he lived in a retirement village in a rural area where I visited every week from the city some hours away. There was no toxic cord between us, but I was aware that my independent dad drew strongly on me for support when he needed it. It was okay with me.

One day, I rang him to see how he was. Alan was quite chirpy, saying he'd just left the front door open and put the lights on for when I arrived. I was puzzled. For one thing, it was mid morning. For another, I was not due to visit for two days, and I always arrived in the morning. I voiced my confusion, which grew when he replied matter-of-factly that I would need to get in that night, when he was in the hospital.

At that point, Alan uttered a loud cry. My heart leaped into my mouth as over the phone line I heard the sound of my father falling and what I assumed was furniture crashing to the floor. Immediately I hung up and called his neighbors, who were able to get to him through his open front door. I then called the ambulance, telling them I'd be there in three hours—the time it would take to drive to the rural hospital. When I arrived at the emergency room, the doctor told me Alan had had a grand mal seizure.

The doctor mentioned that he'd been lucky—if Alan had not had such immediate medical attention he might have died.

While he was kept in the hospital to stabilize, I decided to stay in his villa. Sure enough, when I arrived after dark, the lights were on and the front door unlocked for me to get in.

I have an extensive background in daily meditation practice and had in previous years worked on cutting cords that had controlled me early in my life—among them one with my father. What used to be a relationship that operated on approval, obligation, expectation and resentment became clearer, full of love and mutual respect. The current connection between Alan and myself was not a toxic, compulsive cord, but on a level which allowed me to tune in to him and sense how he was, at will. Used to following the subtle prompts of my Higher Self I had called my father just before the precise moment he had needed me. His own precognition, however, was not his normal state. As has been documented in medical literature, his brain had been stimulated to extraordinary awareness by the electrical activity that is a precursor of a grand mal seizure.

A few years later, my beloved father died. I continued the at-will connection to him long after he had left his body. It is very real to me that death is no separation, and that we do not need cords to maintain a sense of a beloved other.

Chapter 17

Strange phenomena

There are some peculiar phenomena we might not at first realize are due to cords. Apart from the toxic connections that can develop between parent and child, lovers and friends, there are many other types of cords that can attach us to our pets, to places and to our possessions. Just as we can imprint positive or negative energy on other people, we can develop unhealthy attachments to inanimate things.

WHAT NO ONE TELLS YOU
ABOUT SPECIAL POSSESSIONS

A "transitional object" is a special possession such as a stuffed toy or blanket that a child uses to connect with feelings of safety and security while undergoing a stressful transition, such as weaning or going to kindergarten for the first time.[16] As the child matures, they have less need for transitional objects, though in times of great stress they will still rely on them to feel secure.

As adults, we can use photographs, jewelry or other mementos for the same purpose. We can create transitional objects out of everyday things—a pressed flower, a theater ticket from a magical first date. When we make a talisman of an object, perhaps significant only to us, we believe it will keep us safe. A transitional object ceases to have its original function and takes on the significance of what it represents—a loving relationship or a feeling of being protected. It illustrates how we use energetic attachments such as cords.

Alistair, a young man on his first long solo overseas trip to a foreign country as an exchange student, took with him his favorite coffee mug. It had been a gift from a girlfriend who died tragically young. Now, he's a veteran foreign correspondent who is regularly sent on assignment to the world's trouble spots. Whether in a war zone or disaster region, his mug functions as a talisman that he takes with him everywhere he goes. To him, it's a sacred object and a necessity. The mug, in fact, stands as a constant reminder of his sweetheart and his great loss. He reveres her memory to the point where no living girl could ever measure up to her. Twenty years later, he remains a bachelor and will be so until he can let the memory of his forlorn love go.

Claire kept a solid gold locket from an old boyfriend, telling herself it was too valuable to throw away. Secretly, however, she was drawing on its energy exactly as she had when, as a child, she had lugged her stuffed toy lamb with her. She strongly felt it was a last connection to him, even though it was clear he was no longer interested in a relationship with her. Somehow it was comforting. It took years before she realized she was actively holding herself back by keeping the locket. She gave it away and moved on, having learned how to hold on to her Self instead.

Coralie's mother left her antique jewelry to her daughter when she died. When the younger woman was feeling nostalgic or lonely, she would take it out and wear it. Inevitably Coralie assumed a Tragic Romantic Character, cloaking everything she saw with sentimentality and regret for the past. When she realized there was a link between what she was feeling and the energy carried in the jewelry, she was aghast at the thought of having to get rid of her precious heirlooms. It wasn't necessary. She had the precious stones and old gold settings carefully cleaned, and some reset. It made a significant difference when she next wore them. Just in case there is still some energetic transfer, though, Coralie makes sure that she doesn't wear the jewelry for long periods of time.

A transitional object can also be very helpful when we use it to reconnect ourselves to positive feelings of being completely accepted or unconditionally loved, and can then spread this over the rest of our life. We can actually make a transitional object out of a memory that conveys peace and love.

Therese had undergone the horrendous trauma of an attempt on her life by an ex-boyfriend. Feeling more vulnerable on a daily basis than she believed possible, she became even more afraid as the offender neared the time of release. Apart from clearing cords to this man, one of the most significant elements of her healing process was to remember Harlan, her first love, from when she was 16. At that time, she had been completely in the moment, loving and loved. The memory reminded her of who she really is and gave her strength and empowerment to deal proactively with all the current challenges in her life. After some time, she no longer needed the stepping stone of her transitional object—the memory of Harlan—to feel she really was strong, safe and in control of her own life.

CLUTTERING UP YOUR LIFE WITH OLD TIES

How many of us hoard personal belongings like jewelry, books, CDs, photographs and mementos? Attachment to our stuff can weigh us down. Every book or music CD that has "sentimental" value, every photo that has a memory, every piece of clothing that has a story, the energy we have given to our belongings takes us out of present time and into the past, where unresolved situations and relationships lurk.

If we regularly cull our clutter—selling, recycling, giving away or throwing out anything that is no longer of use—our whole energy is cleaner, as less of it is tied up in the past. When we declutter, as well as clearing up our homes, we free up personal energy to use in pursuit of an active, fulfilling life and our dreams.

MUSICAL CONNECTIONS

Music, in particular, can take us out of present time, carrying with it a particular mood or the atmosphere of a bygone era, the fashions of the time and social customs, some of which we might nostalgically wish we could return to. Sometimes this is fun—a way of visiting the past and remembering good times. At times, however, it can drain us of energy and make us less effective in the present, particularly if it comes with a romantic fantasy of old times being the best times, or if the energy it creates does not match what we are doing in our lives right now. Music also has extraordinary power to inspire and thrill us, restore and soothe us or energize us as needed. It depends on how we use it.

These days, the ability to keep music digitally means that space is far less of a problem than it was when the only way we could keep our favorite music was in bulging racks of vinyl records. As technology rapidly advanced it wasn't unusual for people to have the same albums in three or four different formats simultaneously—records, audio tapes and on CD, along with the equipment to play them— and then in digital storage systems. Each hard copy of an album, however, is valuable to those who keep them precisely because of its physical representation of an older time.

This is not a bad thing—sometimes the totality of the music is included not only in the sound but in the cover, like the world of a book we hold in our hands, with the very real feel and smell of the paper and the pages we turn. The more murky energy of the past is not carried on media manufactured in more modern materials. A CD and its cover might pull us back sentimentally to the past, but its energy is not as loaded as a vinyl record produced 50 years ago. In a digital format we get only the energy of the music and its pulling power. It's not a problem if we are aware to what degree we are pulled out of the present by these things, and can bring ourselves back to be as effective as we can when we need to be.

AM I FEEDING AN UNHEALTHY CONNECTION?

When we leave our belongings at a friend's place—seemingly by accident—it can often be a subtle indication that we have a cord to that person. Energetically, we have left a marker, not unlike an animal marking its territory. By these "droppings," we are also unconsciously reinforcing the cord or attachment. To a degree we are allowing our energy to "leak." We can form cords in this way simply because our personal boundaries are not clear and strong.

Sally and Jenna were roommates who occasionally shared clothes and accessories, as well as living space. They felt they were more like sisters than friends. When Jenna went to a university in another state, many of their belongings were intermingled. They continued to wear favorite pieces of each other's clothing while other clothes stayed in boxes for over a year. They laughingly acknowledged that one day they'd have to sort them all out, but they weren't particularly worried about it.

In the beginning their almost daily contact by phone, texting or e-mail allowed them to feel part of each other's lives. This contact gradually became less frequent. Then, Sally became depressed over a breakup with a boyfriend and, inexplicably, Jenna also began experiencing overwhelming sadness, loss of interest in her surroundings, insomnia and lack of energy. Neither of them had any idea that the strong cord between them—begun in friendship and genuine caring—also carried negative emotions.

They didn't realize that keeping each other's clothes and accessories in their wardrobes was helping to maintain an unhealthy connection even when they were talking less frequently. Sally was unaware she was sending her sadness to Jenna through the cord that connected them, which was reinforced by shared belongings. At least part of the problem was a lack of personal boundaries. Had they learned how to share their lives without taking on board other people's issues, and simultaneously sorted out whose physical belongings belonged to whom, they would have been more effective and better friends to each other.

A SNAPSHOT OF THE PAST

Photographs are precious reminders of happy times and past relationships with loved ones who have died or moved away. This is why house fires and other disasters that destroy personal mementos can be so devastating. However, we can unconsciously maintain toxic cords when we keep photographs and keepsakes of past hurtful or problematic relationships. We need to ask ourselves why we're still keeping these old memories—which are effectively repositories of pain and regret. The energy around them is invariably stagnant and can prevent us from moving on. Not every cherished photograph will have this effect on us, but some will. Have a look at your photo albums. What effect may keeping each of them be having on you?

BAD DEBTS

A debt not only ties up our future earnings, it also ties us to the person to whom we owe money. It's a good reason to discharge any debts we have incurred as soon as possible—especially to friends or family. What began as a free flow of good will and generosity often morphs into bad feeling and regret.

The longer a debt with a friend or family member exists unredeemed or unforgiven, the stronger a cord becomes. It's not only money that's tied up in a debt, but our attention and expectations. If our expectation of being repaid is not honored, a cord with our bad debtor can fill with disappointment, resentment and even hatred. It's reinforced every time we think of them. This can result in the flow of our creative energy being blocked, as we try to suppress all these bad feelings.

And, if we're caught in a trap of not repaying a debt we have incurred, it's a common human reaction to find our former good opinion of our lender deteriorating. Whenever we do wrong by someone and do not rectify it as soon as possible—including repaying a debt—certain aspects of that person, even a friend, become objectionable in our eyes. Eventually we might convince ourselves we have every right not to repay the money we owe. We begin to blame them for imagined slights or bad character traits. We might irrationally consider that, in fact, they don't deserve to be repaid.

Though unwarranted, our negative emotions flow from us along a cord to the one who has done us a favor in lending us money. And then, of course, we might also receive the intensified bad feelings of our creditor along the cord, as well.

If we realize in time that we really do not need more negativity flowing into our energy field, affecting how we think and feel, we'll make every effort to repay our debt—or be paid—as soon as possible. Whenever we pay a bill or a debt, we free the creative flow of fresh energy into our lives once more. Opportunities, good fortune and positive connections result.

ANIMAL COMPANIONS

Like humans, animals have an astral and etheric body. Unlike us, they do not have an Egoic body. It means that their emotions are unbounded and untempered by rationality. The strong emotional connection between animal companions and their human family means that, through cords, an animal will share or be affected by its carer's chronic emotional state. Though it's the last thing we might want to do, unconsciously we can off-load our anxiety on to our beloved pets. Unable to handle this, they become sick, just as we do. In a conversation with animal whisperer Trisha McCagh of www .animaltalk.com, she told me that animals willingly share the burden of their owner's illness as an act of unconditional love.

There've been numerous documented cases of animals finding their owners after they've moved to a new house—sometimes hundreds of miles away. This happens through the cords that link the animal to its human family.

Videotaped experiments with intentional thought have shown that at the exact time a person begins their return journey home, their beloved pet responds by going to wait at a window, door or gate, tail wagging, scratching at a door, whining, barking, howling or yowling. Even more telling, some pets become excited when their owner calls from overseas. The animal might go to the phone when the owner is on the other end of the line, but not for any other caller. All of these documented experiments show that the animal's excitement could not be in response to having heard the owner coming, nor by the observer at home knowing beforehand when the owner's arrival is expected.[17] It is quite simply due to telepathy—a word which in Greek is *tele* meaning "far" and *pátheia* meaning "feeling," from the same root as empathy or sympathy. If seen from an evolutionary perspective, telepathy between animals and others of their species—as well as between animals and humans, and human to human—has an obvious survival value.

The attachments animals have with humans can manifest in all sorts of unusual ways. Vets regularly encounter cases of animals acting out their jealousy of their carer's partner, for example. In dogs, cats and birds, jealousy can lead to anxious overgrooming, as well as aggressive, attacking behavior toward their perceived rival. There are many stories in the media of animals alerting other people when their owner is injured or ill, or actually rescuing their owner. There have also been cases when a pet's intervention has prevented their owner from committing suicide. Much of this is due to a loving connection that is an energetic cord.

Likewise, through a cord, an animal in need will reach out over distance to its owner for help with a particular kind of urgency that feels exactly like the effect of a distressed howl or a yowl for attention, or scratching at a door. When an animal is lost and wants to be found, it can telepathically communicate where it is, though often the images that come along the cord are not recognizable to their owner.

A cord with an animal is unlike one with another human. It lacks emotional baggage—at least from the animal's side. Like its vocal communication, cord transmissions from an animal are often brief and purposeful. The exception is when they pine over a period of time. Though painfully intense and distressing on occasion, it's still nothing like the fermented nastiness of a cord with another human being who is simply off-loading unwanted emotions. We can harm a pet with our emotional baggage. An animal lacks the boundaries not to be affected by whatever emotions or energy come through cords from their owners. This can include inheriting some of our illnesses.

If you're in doubt about the connection between you and your cat or dog, think loving thoughts about them, without speaking, while you're in the same room. They will usually respond with a purr or a wag of a tail, or look up with a sweet expression as they feel, and return, your love.

BOUND BY PLACES

Just as we become unhealthily attached to people and things, we can develop cords to places—whether it is our childhood home, a vacation destination or even a workplace.

Drew had a cord to the first house he had designed and built. A self-styled greenie conservationist, he lived by the tenets of sustainable energy. The house was in a rural area, made out of hand-pressed mud bricks and sandstone blocks he'd quarried himself, with handmade stained-glass windows and carved door frames. A great deal of Drew's youthful joy, creative energy and idealism, as well as blood, sweat and tears, had gone into the house. He felt he'd left something of himself in the very walls and fabric of the place.

Drew's children had been raised in the house and he'd lived there with his wife for 20 years before she left him, suddenly, for another man. Drew had already cleared the bitter cord he'd had to his ex-wife. As for the house itself, he'd not lived there for 10 years, having rented it out to a succession of short-term tenants. Some of them had talked of the house being haunted—which Drew found perplexing, as no one had died there.

Finally he decided it was time to sell, but despite the rapid growth in real estate prices in his area, it seemed no one was interested in buying his unique, beautiful house. Then Drew realized that his attachment to the house was based on a forlorn hope that somehow he'd get back his youthful idealism and happiness.

Was it coincidence that a week after he'd cleared the cord to the house, a buyer made a good offer? This man was interested in making it into a bed & breakfast, capitalizing on its highly desirable sustainable-technology features. Drew realized that he'd been reluctant to sell before because of a fear that it would be torn down. He'd felt this would in turn mean his whole life would become rubble. Completing the sale, Drew gladly moved on to the next chapter in his life.

A CURSED PRACTICE

My dentist took me aside one day and asked if I would do a clearing on her office. There were three things she was concerned about. One was a strong energetic presence belonging to the now-retired founder of the practice, still palpably evident in the room he had always used. No one in the practice wanted to be in that room. In another room there was an energetic imprint of a patient, a friend of the current dentist, who had suicided. The third concern affected the entire practice: a former receptionist had left in a resentful, disgruntled state and had put a curse on the office.

My dentist is a rational person, but sensitive and aware of subtle energies. We picked a time when patients had left for the day and I opened my awareness to sense what might be toxic cords from these three people.

The room that had been exclusively used by the original dentist was full of his strong energy. A powerful, generous and creative man, but quick to anger, often intimidating those unable to stand up to his belligerence, his life force had maintained the practice against a great deal of opposition from colleagues for many years. In the second room there was some sadness, due to the dentist's regret over her friend's suicide. I felt the cord was more of an association she had had with him, imprinted on the space, the last place she had seen him. As for the curse that was affecting the whole practice, I noticed a subtle undermining energy in the office, not from anyone currently there, but in artwork on the walls, which exerted a sour influence on patients and staff alike. The dentist confirmed that the former receptionist had chosen the décor of the office and all that remained of her choices were the hanging paintings.

I set up the ritual and cleared the two rooms and the curse over the whole practice. Two months later she remarked that the practice was busier than it had ever been and she had to hire extra dentists and nursing staff to cope with appointments. The practice continues to thrive, the happy faces of the staff showing how much they all enjoy working there.

Chapter 18

Seriously toxic—
personality disorders

To a large extent, it is the quality of our parenting that determines how healthily we are able to relate. A deprived, neglected, abused or smothered child has at the base of their personality structure either a broken or fused connection that creates a separation panic or abandonment depression so profound that the emergence of a real Self may not occur.[18] This can create pathological disorders of the Self.[19] I will only touch briefly on these in order to help identify when we might find ourselves in a relationship with one such damaged soul.

When we encounter these individuals we might at first think they are perfectly normal people, since they often camouflage what they are. Alternatively, we might think they are simply examples of some of the more difficult Characters we come across in life, not realizing how extremely toxic cords with them might become. Some psychological conditions run in families. Research suggests this can be due to genetic predisposition or altered brain chemistry, but it's also because damaged parents inevitably damage their children. Every relationship becomes an arena for unconscious destructive games, as the illusions within which the disordered Self lives—a nightmare fantasy universe—are projected onto everyone in the environment. Distortions arising from a sense of entitlement, grandiosity and paranoia can mean that criminal acts such as abuse or rape are part of the picture.

Lest we judge or condemn, be aware that, to a degree, all of us may share some of these wounded states. The disorders of the Self are best seen on a continuum rather than as discrete or isolated conditions. Like every human being they deserve compassion and kindness, but in some cases the best and safest course of action for us is to walk away. We do not help by allowing ourselves to be victimized.

RISING ABOVE ABUSE

In their late 50s, childless couple and former professional dancers Kevin and Amanda had a dancing academy and were convinced that their teaching and choreography were the best in the city. They regularly congratulated themselves and their young dancers on how lucky they were to be in their "dancing family." Trophies and awards the youngsters won were never allowed to go home with the winners. They were proudly displayed at the studio as though Kevin and Amanda had won them. One talented student, 14-year-old Fiona, was almost an adopted daughter. She had been at the academy since she was six and by this time taught all the littlest ones.

Amanda was their Mother Hen, solicitous over the students' health and welfare and often interfering in their home and family life to make sure dancing, and the academy, were their first priority.

When Fiona announced she had a won a scholarship to a national dance school, Amanda made frantic attempts to keep their unpaid teacher-trainee. It then came to light that Kevin had a dark secret.

Since Fiona was eight years of age Kevin had been sexually abusing her.

On this being made public, many of the younger girls came forward, backed by their mothers, saying they, too, had been molested on a regular basis. Before this, none of the students had dared reveal the secret, through a combination of confusion, misguided loyalty to Amanda and fear of Kevin.

A complex web of toxic cords underlay this situation. Kevin was a psychopathic narcissist. A self-vaunted master choreographer, he alternated erratic praise with devastating, unfair criticism to undermine the confidence of his dancers. At the same time he was privately telling the youngsters that his sexual attention was a special, secret favor to which they alone were entitled. Each of his victims was bound to him by uncertainty, secrecy and fear, and the neediness he fostered and exploited.

Apparently unaware of Kevin's extracurricular activities, Amanda's main emotional response to the girls was also alternately approval and criticism, edged with cold demands that they try harder. Both Kevin and Amanda expected total dedication and loyalty from their students.

When Amanda found out about the sexual abuse, she made sure everyone knew she was outraged at the allegations and defended Kevin with outright lies. A few angry parents took their children away, but others, notably those whose children had not been abused, rallied to Amanda's side, and the young dancers were determined to help her keep the academy together.

When Kevin was sent to jail, Amanda's Mother Hen Character

became tinged with a bitter energy that covertly blamed the young dancers—and in particular Fiona, now away at the national dance school—for the disaster. This bitterness fed every cord she had with them. She seemed not to be able to help herself, often reducing dancers to tears during classes.

Before long, classes diminished and Amanda barely had any candidates for the dance competitions that had played such a large part in their calendar. The resentment that now flowed from Amanda into cords she had carefully nurtured with their former dancers soured the entire academy until it had to close.

For most of the young dancers who were entangled in the abusive cords of this elaborate web of self-serving control, it took years to reestablish self-esteem and confidence. As long as she lived, Amanda had a habit of poring over the many old photograph albums of the academy in its happier days, spending a moment or two looking at every student in angry self-pity and blame. Every emotion was a dart of venom to a former loyal student. At the same time, her denial of any wrong-doing on Kevin's part allowed her to idolize him as a hero cruelly wronged, and to see his accusers as enemies who had viciously attacked him for reasons of jealousy. When Kevin was killed in jail by another inmate, this idealizing of her husband grew to legendary proportions.

Meanwhile, regardless of the talent that had won Fiona a scholarship, her confidence remained shaky and as an adult she never quite made it as a professional dancer. She returned to her hometown to find Amanda ill and almost destitute. Fiona's misguided loyalty and guilt, fed by the strong attachment she had to Amanda, gave her the idea to set up a new dance school for children under both her and Amanda's names. With the chance of a return to her former spotlight, Amanda accepted, conveniently forgetting the blame she had formerly heaped on Fiona.

Initially the new school flourished with the energy Fiona was pouring into it, but Amanda's poisonous influence remained. In the studio, an aging, arthritic Amanda sat in the corner with her cane, like a venomous spider, rasping out stinging criticism and complaints and interrupting Fiona's classes to advise her protégée and Rescuer on how to keep her students in line. Fiona had been well-conditioned. She was unable to distinguish verbal abuse from discipline and the genuine guiding benevolence of a teacher. Feeling wretchedly inadequate, Fiona in turn slipped into creating abusive cord relationships with each new swatch of hopeful young dancers, under the seeming care of her next-generation "dancing family."

Amanda's mental state had been deteriorating into dementia for some time before it became obvious that the school could not continue. Her irrational, vitriolic outbursts struck wildly, regardless of whether they fell on hapless young students trying their best, or loyal Fiona, smoothing over a parent's indignation. Becoming more frail, the aging Amanda fell one day and broke her hip. In the hospital she raged over being put into the geriatric ward while Fiona ran the dwindling dance school without Amanda's intrusive overview.

Fiona had been in therapy for some time for depression and anxiety, but it was only when it became clear that Amanda would not be returning to the school that she began to realize the hold both Amanda and the now-dead Kevin still had on her through their toxic cords. Extensive therapy and many cord clearings later, Fiona still has to struggle with the restrictions of her early conditioning on occasion, but feels she is beginning to find her Self for the first time.

SURVIVING RAPE

Rape is rarely about sex. It's much more often about power, hatred and control. Behind that, is fear.

Aisha was a sweet-faced, timid soul in her 20s with multiple phobias. One of the main symptoms was agoraphobia. She could not go out, even in the company of friends or family, unless it was for a brief period of time and she was coming home straight afterward. She was obsessive about cleanliness, to the point where she washed her hands 50–60 times whenever she went to the bathroom. Her fear of germs extended to a terror of contamination from her own urine, excrement and menstrual flow. She believed she was dirty, and that inside, both physically and morally, she was full of filth.

Aisha was convinced she had been raped as a child and repressed the memory, and this was confirmed by both a psychic and a kinesiologist. Her doctor, however, assured her she was a virgin.

Aisha came to me for a series of regression sessions and we began the gentle process of uncovering the long past event she was sure she had blocked out. It took weeks but eventually she felt safe enough to go into an experience that she had never before had. She described something soft, dark and oppressive enclosing her. It was suffocating. Feeling powerless and afraid, she was unable to escape and squirmed as she related what she was seeing.

She was experiencing violation of a brutal kind when she suddenly realized that her mother was there. How could it be? How could her mother simply stand by and allow this to happen to her child? In horror Aisha watched the scene unfolding in her inner eye. Tears seeped below her closed lids as understanding came and her breathing began finally to relax. I brought her gently back to the present, grounding her in physical reality, before she added to the fragments she had shared aloud during the session. It was nothing like what she had imagined had happened. The truth was far stranger, and in a way, worse.

Aisha had not been raped, but her mother, Farah, had. Aisha had been an unborn baby in the womb at the time.

Following this session, Aisha asked her mother if what she had discovered was true. Unprepared for this, Farah was astounded and burst into tears. Wanting to comfort her mother but at the same time transfixed by disgust at the mucus running from her mother's nose, Aisha could only pat her mother's arm awkwardly, automatically, with eyes averted. Then Farah revealed the rest of the tragic story.

Farah was living in her wartorn native country at the time. Her husband was away fighting and Farah had been caught by invading forces and raped violently by two soldiers. She did not know she was pregnant at the time of the attack. The rapists had left her bruised and bleeding in a cellar, where relatives had found her and cared for her.

A few weeks later she and her family escaped the conflict, finding asylum in another country where her husband joined them. Too ashamed to tell him she had been raped and afraid that he would consider her defiled, Farah was also unable to tell him she now had a deep aversion to sex. In her particular cultural setting it was unthinkable to seek counseling or to share personal problems with anyone outside the family. Her own mother impatiently told her to get on with it and do her wifely duty. Farah's shame was compounded with her overwhelming sense of powerlessness and developed into nervous anxiety. Bound by tradition, she submitted to her husband without letting him know that his very touch terrified and disgusted her.

Within her womb, the fetal Aisha felt every time her parents had sex as an assault and absorbed her mother's tense fear and inability to speak out. After she was born and as the child grew, Farah devoted herself to Aisha, keeping her close by her side at all times. Without any other sympathetic outlet, Farah often poured out her heart to her little daughter, sharing inappropriately intimate details about her married life. She was unaware that in her child's eyes she was creating a monster out of her husband—and by extension all men.

Aisha became increasingly hostile toward her father. Every night, when her parents retired to bed, the fear and aversion Farah experienced with her husband traveled along the cord to Aisha. It was this toxicity that formed the basis of Aisha's phobias.

This was the beginning of many clearings of Aisha's cords with her mother and also a very toxic cord with her father. Aisha's enmeshment with her mother's issues was on many layers and many of her phobias were deeply imprinted.

Nevertheless, Aisha feels she made progress in differentiating between her mother's emotions and her own. She is pleased that she is now able to talk to her father without suspicion and realize the love her family have for her. Her agoraphobia is greatly reduced and she is bringing her compulsive washing under control.

A brief round of family therapy shortly after this identified a further layer of complication. Aisha's two younger sisters and their parents spoke of Aisha as always having taken the lion's share of attention. Her problems had been so overwhelming that no one else in the family felt they had any space. In fact, as it emerged, Aisha's problems were not the only ones she battled, but each member of the family, including Aisha, had formed an unconscious, tacit agreement to make her the scapegoat for everything that was wrong, spotlighting her and diverting blame and frustration onto her instead of dealing with their own issues. A somber realization sat on the family members as they left the session room, while Aisha absorbed the knowledge that in her Victim Character she had somehow agreed to become the garbage disposal for her family's collective unwanted emotions.

Following this, Farah finally allowed herself therapy to heal the wounds of her past. She had long suspected the gynecological problems she had suffered derived from an energetic deposit from her wartime rapists—a toxic cord that still bound her to them. At the same time she had tried to rationalize that such a thing was impossible, a ridiculous fancy. She was confused. She felt this confusion as raw, corrosive fear that she carried in her pelvis—her fear certainly, but also their fear. How could they have been afraid, when they had overpowered her so easily?

There is a curious aspect to many regressions. The person reliving the event can experience not only their own emotions, but also those of others in the situation, from a somewhat detached viewpoint as though floating above those in the event. It is therefore possible to understand a great deal more about a traumatic incident than when we first experience it, although this can be years later, in therapy, when we are ready, and strong enough, to deal with old buried emotions. This time, however, we have the advantage of much greater wisdom and perspective to accompany the uncovering of a painful memory. The shock of the event can be discharged as we see what was happening, on many levels.

In the regression Farah saw that they were young men, minimally trained and inwardly terrified of the chaotic violence around them. Aggression was their way of dealing with their fear, and in that dark cellar long ago they had dumped it all on Farah in a twisted attempt to feel powerful in one area at least. The intensity of the event had allowed cords full of anger, fear and hatred to form. The repercussions on Farah had maintained these toxic connections for decades.

Finally the cords were gone.

Farah decided to follow up her clearings with a course in assertiveness. To her surprise, her husband was fully supportive. Communication has improved between them and Farah describes their relationship as "completely new." In fact, without these venomous cords, the entire family now relates differently.

CHAOS RULES

A cord with a person with a personality disorder is particularly full of vitriol. It is essential for a person in partnership with someone who is suffering from this kind of disorder to detach from the sufferer's samskaras and the highly toxic energy they create. There is evidence to show that with a sincere commitment to heal, these fractured Selves may over time become whole, healthy and real, but treatment is rarely effective if it is not initiated by the person themselves. If you are about to enter into a relationship with, or are already partnered with someone who has a disorder of the Self, you need to know exactly what you are up against.

If your partner polarizes family and friends into those who violently loathe them and those who understand their underlying fragility and try to help them, it may be that they have a Borderline Personality Disorder. Bewilderingly, their neediness for our attention can switch without apparent reason or warning to blaming us for every problem in their life. We can be manipulated unawares by their volatile emotions and as a result our own certainty, confidence and self-esteem can become crippled. Fearing always that they will be left alone and desperately afraid of the emptiness that hides beneath their armored defenses, a person with borderline personality will use emotional blackmail, blame, illness and self-harm to control others. In a relationship with this person we may realize nothing is ever enough and that what pleased them yesterday could very well displease them today. We might always feel on the back foot. This person's defenses are erected anew every instant and we might constantly feel that the relationship is as real as a ghost ship from which we are about to be thrown into the sea.

At the same time, the borderline personality structure entails an inherent split with the real Self, which means they can readily see another's point of view. They are often well-informed about psychology and self-help as a means of keeping the power of that knowledge for themselves, to avoid the shame of allowing another person to see into them first. They can apply self-lacerating insight into their own failings on the one hand, while for long periods are seemingly unable to effect lasting change in their behavior, causing intense frustration and helplessness in close partners and family. If a person with this disorder of the Self can apply their insight without blame, they are capable of healing themselves and eventually becoming whole. It takes enormous courage and creativity, both of which are often part of this person's resources in deep measure.

A person with Histrionic Personality Disorder can be an attention-seeking Drama Queen of either sex who sucks attention and life force from everyone around them wherever they are. Even some houseplants die after a few days in close proximity.

The Drama Queen's neediness is expressed with dramatic outrage and despair. They experience constant hopeful expectations, disappointments and betrayals with an apparent lack of insight as to the cause and effect of these scenarios, and refuse to take a healthier or more realistic attitude. Their misery is palpable and they seem to wallow in it, imposing on others for sympathy and support. Those with experience with them frequently reject them in ways that devastate them, breaking their heart each time in a vicious circle of victimhood. In turn, they reject everyone unless they are able to serve their needs, and criticize others for having priorities other than being there for them.

Their communication is often confusing and mysterious. They'll begin a sentence, carefully eyeing the person they are addressing to see if they are creating the effect they desire. If the response is not as they'd like it, they switch to another line of conversation, confusing their listeners and allowing them to complain that they are constantly misunderstood. They create cords by leaving belongings, carelessly, with friends and recent acquaintances.

They make sure they have a range of friends they can call on. Even when these long-suffering folk are there for them, the Drama Queen drains them so quickly that these friends often do not feel their efforts are matched.

The trap for the histrionic disordered person is always to use their flamboyance to attract external kudos for the approval they so desperately need. Through creativity, however, they can express—and thereby create—the true Self. Only when they can find love of Self through acknowledging their own worth will they begin to heal.

A person with a narcissistic personality structure may act out their denial of their abandonment depression with grandiose ideas, a sense of entitlement that means one set of rules for themselves and another for everyone else, constant lies, a need for constant adoration (called "narcissistic supply") and lack of empathy. We can frequently see examples in professional athletes, performers, CEOs or politicians. These individuals desire fame, which feeds their fantasies about themselves. A narcissistic person might fabricate achieve-ments, personal history and honors with no basis in fact, but believe it all utterly.

They will often feel nauseated by affection and affinity that is not directed toward themselves. However, they can mimic these quali-ties to manipulate a target they want to control and dominate. In a subordinate position they will undermine the integrity of a superior by favors, gifts and work beyond the call of duty. The intention is to ingratiate themselves and compromise the targeted person higher in the hierarchy. In a boss, however, the narcissistic structure demands complete and devoted loyalty, and often expects extra favors and gifts as their due. They are erratic in promotion and punishment of underlings with little regard to their actual worth, enjoying the un-ease of staff at their unpredictability. At the same time, they believe they are at the beck and call of others, in their service. If we have a cord with this person, all these emotional states are intensified and we can sometimes be wrongly convinced they are right, while we are wrong.

If you are in a romantic relationship with someone with a Narcis-sistic Personality Disorder, you might find they engage in serial infi-delity as though entitled, while demanding complete fidelity from you, without any insight into the devastation this causes to a partner-ship. In a marriage, the narcissist demands that their spouse mirror exactly their opinions. There is no room for another opinion or point of view, and so the person who can stay married to a narcissist is often a co-narcissist. This is the function of a courtier, pacifier or booster for the narcissist, defending their partner against "unreason-able" or "demanding" relatives, making sure they are happy and kept in narcissistic supply. Such partners ignore their own wishes or dreams in subservience of their spouse, citing loyalty but really putting their partner's happiness always ahead of their own. Think of *The Simpsons'* Charles Montgomery Burn's devoted executive assistant, Waylon Smithers, as an example. The cord between such a couple is often so fused that the co-narcissist defends their partner's behavior, even when patently wrong.

The above descriptions are typical of the most commonly identifiable forms of narcissism—the exhibitionist and the co-narcissist—but there is another kind of narcissist, called a "closet narcissist," who draws attention to themselves by being overly self-deprecating, self-loathing, submissive and compliant. They will idealise a partner and identify or fuse with them, in which circumstances they can be highly capable and high functioning. However, idealism soon fades and disappointment sets in. It is extremely difficult for these sufferers to maintain lasting intimate relationships and they manifest a high degree of eating disorders, compulsions, alcoholism or drug dependency to avoid the depths of their abandonment depression.[20]

TAKING RESPONSIBILITY

For a person with a disorder of the Self, taking responsibility for their emotions and the consequences of their actions might be extremely difficult if not impossible. Though a relationship with a person with a personality disorder can leave us feeling shredded, deeply hurt, angry and bewildered, in the end it takes much less energy for us to take responsibility for our own emotions than to blame them and seethe with hatred and resentment. Remember, too, that in a cord, the emotions we're feeling are often not even ours.

Taking responsibility for our own emotions doesn't mean we become more selfish or run away to avoid helping someone else. It means we know honestly what we can do and what we can't. We can avoid making promises we might not be able to keep. The fact that a person with a personality disorder cannot maintain an equal, reciprocal relationship and is unable to bring the fullness of Self to meet a partner, might mean that the healthiest thing we can do in such a situation is to walk away, without blame.

FATAL FLAWS

In his excellent, fascinating and readable book *Fatal Flaws*, psychiatrist and professor Stuart C. Yudofsky, of the Baylor College of Medicine in Houston, Texas, has detailed the personality disorders that cause tragedies and ravage lives and relationships. To help us identify a person who might have a disorder of the Self—as differentiated from mere personality or character flaws—he has devised the Fatal Flaw Scale.[21] I reproduce it here in full with his kind permission and that of American Psychiatric Publishing Inc. If you are at all unsure about the person you are about to enter a relationship with, or are already partnered by, it is a useful checklist.

The fatal flaw scale

PART A
Does this person have a personality and/or character flaw?

Please check the best answer, "Yes" or "No," to the following questions regarding the person with whom you have an important relationship. If you are not sure, mark that answer "No."

1. Do I trust this person? (Yes) (No)

2. Has this person "come through" on important commitments? (Yes) (No)

3. Do I feel better about myself as a consequence of this relationship? (Yes) (No)

4. Does this person consider my needs equally to his or hers? (Yes) (No)

5. Is this person sensitive to and supportive of me? (Yes) (No)

6. Will this person communicate with me honestly on significant issues affecting our relationship? (Yes) (No)

7. Is this person honest with other people and trustworthy in his or her relationships? (Yes) (No)

8. Do I, and (if applicable) do my children, always feel physically safe with this person? (Yes) (No)

9. Does this person respect rules and obey laws? (Yes) (No)

10. Do other people whom I love and trust the most believe this person is good for me? (Yes) (No)

DIRECTIONS: Total the number of "No" answers that you checked.

SCORING:

A. 0 "No": Highly Unlikely that this person has flaws of personality and character.

B. 1–3 "No": Possible that this person has flaws of personality and character.

C. 4–5 "No": Probable that this person has flaws of personality and character.

D. 6–10 "No": Highly Likely that this person has flaws of personality and character.

PART B
Does this person's flaws of personality and character qualify as being a *fatal* flaw?

(Only to be determined if score on Part A is 4 or higher.)

Please check the best answer, "Yes" or "No," to the following questions regarding the person with whom you have an important relationship. For questions 1, 2 and 3, if you are not sure, mark that answer "Yes." If you do not have access to accurate information regarding questions 4, 5 and 6, do not check an answer.

1. Does this person insist on engaging in activities that are impulsive, unnecessarily dangerous or self-destructive? (Yes) (No)

2. Does this person deny that he or she has a problem? (Yes) (No)

3. Does this person refuse professional help for their problem? (Yes) (No)

4. Does this person's problem remain unchanged despite many courses of professional help? (Yes) (No)

5. Is there a good chance that, in the future, this person will physically injure me or my child? (Yes) (No)

6. Does this person persist in engaging in illegal acts? (Yes) (No)

DIRECTIONS: Total the number of "Yes" answers that you checked.

SCORING:

A. 0 "Yes": Highly Unlikely that this person has a fatal flaw.

B. 1–2 "Yes": Possible that this person has a fatal flaw.

C. 3–4 "Yes": Probable that this person has a fatal flaw.

D. 5–6 "Yes": Highly Likely that this person has a fatal flaw.

Note: If you find yourself in a relationship with someone who scored Highly Likely to have a fatal flaw in the Fatal Flaw Scale, know that it is rarely possible to maintain a healthy partnership with such a person.[22]

Subtle body awareness exercise 2: Experiencing the astral body

To continue the subtle body awareness exercise at the end of Part 1, this practice focuses on the astral body.

1. Sit facing a partner about an arms-length away and close your eyes. Become aware of your breathing. As you breathe in, life force enters your body and fills your lungs. It is carried in your blood and fills every muscle, tissue and organ in your body. It renews your body energy with every inhalation. As you breathe out the old, used air, you're also letting go of tension, relaxing a little bit more with every out-breath. This happens without your needing to make it happen, and you can use it as a way of letting go with intention, to release old thoughts and ideas, old emotions, anything you might be holding on to that you no longer need. Now, settle into your body, feeling it from the inside. See if you can increase how comfortable you feel within your own space.

2. Still with yourself, establish a baseline for how you are feeling in your body. Use inner sensing to feel how you are in general, in terms of relaxation, mood, energy level. Can you feel any areas of tension in your body? Any areas of congestion that may not be purely physical? Spend a few moments relaxing by intention, using the out-breath to let go of whatever you no longer need to hold on to.

3. When you feel relatively comfortable within your own body, open your eyes. Without speaking, gently tune in to the other person. Without

intruding, take in how they seem to be in an emotional sense. Take time to create a space of acceptance and receptivity between you, observing without judgment, feeling how they feel by what emotions you feel, by perhaps, what happens to your breathing. Be open. If momentary self-consciousness makes you laugh, let that happen until it passes, and simply relax looking at each other in gentle, nonstaring eye contact. Match your breathing to the other person's, so you are breathing in synchrony. Silently share the space you are in. After a few minutes, verbally share your impressions with your partner.

4. Now, close your eyes again and become aware of your heart. By this I mean your etheric heart in the center of your chest, rather than your physical heart. Spend a few silent moments tuning in to your own heart and how it feels. Then open your eyes, become aware of the other person's heart. Tune in to how their heart feels, how it is different from yours. Share the heart space between you without speaking for a while. How does it feel compared to the previous exercise? Take some time, enjoy the warmth and acceptance of this heart space. Then listen to your partner's impressions and tell them yours.

5. Close your eyes again and drop your awareness to your belly, the area just below your navel. Again, silently tune in to your own first. How does it feel? Compare it to how your heart felt. Spend a few moments there until you have some sense of how your belly feels. Open your eyes and without speaking become aware of the other person's belly, feeling differences and similarities between you. With gentle eye contact, still matching your breathing, silently share the belly space and compare how it feels, different from the heart space. After a few minutes, tell your partner your impressions.

6. Close your eyes once more and focus your attention between your eyebrows. This is the Third Eye space, and depending on whether you have practiced this in meditation, you will see, feel and experience quite different things here. It's also different each time—so there is nothing anyone should be seeing or feeling here. It can become quite intense, so it's important not to use any effort. Simply relax and hold a gentle awareness between your eyebrows, becoming aware of how it feels there, different from the heart and the belly space. Open your eyes, become aware of the other person's Third Eye without staring and without focusing your eyes between the other person's eyebrows. Share the Third Eye space in silent eye contact. Allow your physical vision to go out of focus. What do you notice? After a few minutes of this, share your impressions out loud with your partner.

7. Now open your awareness to all three energy centers—heart, belly and Third Eye. Become aware of how you feel as you sense the person opposite you. Feel the differences between you with complete acceptance and without judgment. Is the person opposite you centered between all the energy centers or are they more "in" one center than the others? What about you? Are you more in one than the other? See if you can open your awareness in a balanced way throughout heart, belly and Third Eye. It will take a little practice and you may need to repeat this exercise many times.

8. The next exercise involves using intention as an act of will to affect the energy between yourself and your partner. Standing up, face your partner about two arms-lengths away. Feeling the other's energy, see if this distance is comfortable for you. If not, move closer or further apart until you both feel comfortable, while still facing each other. Designate one of you "A" and the other "B." Starting with A, and holding

eye contact without moving, speaking or using any obvious body language or gestures, have an intention to push your partner away.

Notice how, exactly, you are doing that. Is it a push from the Third Eye, the heart or the belly? What happened? Did B move back or stay in the same spot? Exchange impressions and swap, repeat the exercise with B now using silent intention to push A away. Afterward, share your experiences out loud. Note the differences between what happened as either of you did this exercise.

9. In the same position as the previous exercise, stand facing each other at a comfortable distance for you both. Now with A once more, use only silent intention to draw your partner closer. Notice how you are doing it. Reverse roles, and repeat.

   Exchange impressions and experiences. Did your partner move closer? How did that feel? Did either of you focus your attention on any one energy center or did you use all of them equally? What did your partner feel while you were doing this? Now, move to a distance that feels comfortable again. Is it a different distance from the beginning of this exercise?

10. The last exercise in this section involves emotions, one partner at a time. Standing facing B without speaking, A deliberately allows themself to feel fear. You might take your mind back to a situation you remember feeling it in the past. Try not to act afraid or send it up. The more genuinely you can feel and convey the emotion, the energy of fear, the more useful the exercise. B should simply receive without resistance, feeling what A is emoting. After a few minutes, stop, shake it off, exchange impressions. Then B has a turn with the energy of fear.

    Take some time, make sure you shake it off before you start the next emotion, which is anger. While A is silently emoting anger, B should simply allow the energy of anger from A to pass through them in an accepting, nonjudgmental way. Try not to resist the other person's anger, but do observe if you feel the instinctive fight-or-flight impulse within yourself. How does your energy react to this emotion? This is your astral body you are feeling and there will be all sorts of associations with every emotion. Simply be aware of what you feel without resistance and it will pass. After a few moments, stop, shake it off, and exchange your impressions, before swapping.

The next emotion in this exercise is sadness. Again, try not to act it or send it up. The more genuine the emotion the better. Go through the same process with the exercise, remember to let it go completely at the end of each segment, and in the next segment repeat the practice with joyful excitement and finally, admiration.

With each one, make sure you shake it off afterward. After you've been through all these emotions, share your overall impressions. Did you find that some emotions came from one center while others came from others? Did you find yourself in general coming more from one center or all of them?

Astral bodies and awareness

Our astral bodies resonate with one another in all sorts of ways, usually in an emotional way. When you practice awareness of astral flows between you and other people you can feel when there is an energy "dump" or "drain." It's very normal, in fact, it's the way most people interact without even realizing it, but you may not wish to be doing this or feeling it from other people. Awareness of these emotional tugs and flows makes us better able to control our own energy. The energy we feel at such times is always conditioned—meaning it is a reaction based on a previous experience, in the past. We are not in the here and now whenever the baggage of the past informs how we respond to others. Whenever we react emotionally, we are identifying with the energy of the astral body. Because that emotion comes from the past, it is therefore not relevant to what is happening now. Instead, we need to practice being in the present.

If you've practiced the exercises above and those for the etheric body on page 70, you might have noticed that what keeps us most grounded in the present is awareness of the physical universe of solid material objects. If you feel yourself being pulled into an emotional reaction, know that it is informed by some experience of the past, and focus your attention on a physical object in the present. Feel the chair you are sitting in, touch the table or wall near you. Feel the solidity of the material, its temperature and texture. Bring yourself back to the here and now. Breathe. Let yourself respond in the present to what is happening. It will be quite different from your usual reaction.

Part three

The Journey to Healing

IT helps on the way to healing if we focus less on the feeling of being restricted by our cords and more on the fact that, as we become more aware of them, they will hold us back less. And one day, we will stand free and clear with a heart full of joy and gladness for the journey as well as the destination.

Chapter 19

Moving out of the tangle

In the preceding chapters we've looked at the ways energetic cords can complicate relationships. In many cases, though unbearably toxic, they can keep a partnership going long after its natural life cycle.

So, how can we form relationships that allow both partners the freedom and the fun of joining our energy to someone we love in a committed way, with no mind or control games?

SORTING YOURSELF OUT

The first step is to get clear about you. Do you think of yourself mainly as someone's girlfriend or daughter, someone's husband or son, belonging to this organization or that group? Or do you have a strong and clear sense of who you are as an individual? Are you a healthy narcissist, as opposed to a pathological one? That's when you can see both good and bad parts of yourself, but you feel adequate, competent and real. You are concerned for others, but not dependent on them for your self-esteem or happiness. In short, you are whole.

To be a whole, mature person we need to know ourselves as individuals, we need to differentiate. Before we can form healthy partnerships, we need to have a distinct sense of who we are apart from others. We need to be self-defined, which means that our view of ourselves needs to matter more than how others see us. It doesn't mean we can't listen to others' opinions, it means we judge for ourselves how relevant other people's opinions of us are. We need to be—and see ourselves as—independent beings. And for this we need clarity and not self-delusion.

This process starts with seeing who we are not, especially when our behavior is conditioned by past experiences that caused us pain, making us more guarded or manipulative than we would rather be. Finding out who we truly are takes time, observation and patience. We need to be scrupulously honest about ourselves, have a good sense of humor and the ability to let go of our failures.

Our sense of self can often be an elusive thing; we can be easily influenced by strong personalities around us as we are growing up. Who we are can be something we feel, often quite vaguely, as we start to measure our own values, opinions and beliefs against those of other people. As we learn to honor our own values more, our sense of self becomes stronger and more apparent, less able to be wounded by circumstance or unkindness and less determined by others.

If we define ourselves merely by our relationships, our possessions, our family and cultural background and our successes, we are agreeing to be far less than we really are. Watch when you find yourself caring more for what someone else thinks of you than for your own self-knowledge—it means you are losing the differentiation of who you are. Perhaps you find, on ending a relationship, that your ex-partner's interests, job or status were what determined your daily activities and your life, which then changed radically after the split. When this happens, come back to your sense of Self and hold tight to that. Quite apart from our partner's life, we're not our achievements, personal history, status, position, profession, job or relationships. Holding on to any of those things, believing that is who we are, will fail us in the long run. When we create a conscious Self, it ceases to be a default definition and becomes a deliberate creation, an expression of our higher beingness. At this point, our sense of Self should be the only thing we hold on to. The true Self is more amorphous, sometimes elusive, electric, a spark of spirit, a sense of beingness that transcends time and place. And yet, when we feel it, there is a calm certainty, a feeling of truth.

When we approach the task of self-differentiation, like all growth, it happens in stages. As an infant we can't differentiate from our primary caregiver and we are incapable of surviving without their care. As we grow and are able to take care of ourselves more, we need to develop more independence and more personal space. If we don't get this opportunity to find out who we are, we might automatically, and unconsciously, form cords with everyone who is important to us in our life.

Most energetic cords we have with family, lovers, friends and co-workers turn toxic in the end due to our failure to be our own person, to differentiate. Instead, we get locked in to other people's values and expectations and, through the cords, all their baggage as well. In cases of extreme enmeshment, one person might be wholly submissive to or dominating the other. Either way it's an unhealthy way to live. When someone is lost in another person, there is not enough individuality for them to notice the energetic ties that bind one to the other.

The good news is that when we are fully self-determined individuals—or just on the way—we can have relationships that are cord free most of the time. We can create nontoxic cords at will if needed; for example, to sense whether a loved one in another location is safe, well and happy. These cords then dissolve in the natural course of events as long as we're not needy or actively trying to interfere with the other person.

Better still, if we develop the ability to expand our space as a happy, self-empowered individual, we can include others in our space without the need for cords at all, making our space as loving, enriching and sustaining as we can. Including others becomes a matter of intention and we can just as easily reverse the process when we want to be on our own, without the other feeling rejected or excluded.

As well as being clear about who we are, we need to be in the present in our relationships. How many unhealthy pairings or breakups have you heard about that happened because one or both parties held some resentment about a past event that may not even have related to the current relationship?

To be a healthy adult is to be self-determined, self-defined, a whole person comfortable in our own space, our own life in the present, with our own beliefs and values, memories and experiences from which we have learned. When we're living in this empowered way, we can take responsibility for our own well-being and we can relate to others as equals and are able to give and receive freely.

We are truly ourselves when we can listen to others' points of view, their experiences and emotions, without identifying with them and taking those emotions on ourselves, or reactively resisting them; when we can weigh opposing merits and calmly agree or not. Communication skills are important. We are able to explain our own point of view from an equal footing, respectfully and without unnecessary heat. Our ability to listen, empathize and discuss different viewpoints means we're able to sort out complex and at times conflicting situations.

In best-case scenarios, we've been able to face and cope with a variety of unhappy situations as we were growing up. We have learned from them to be stronger and more resourceful, to handle our emotions and allow others to handle theirs. Then, if tragedy or obstacles come our way, we are able to deal with them without necessarily falling into a Victim Character. When we need expert help, we can find it without becoming needy or feeling somehow diminished. Instead, we can take responsibility for ourselves, utilize various appropriate resources and grow through the process.

This means, too, that if someone else tells us their sad story, we can empathize, while allowing them the learning experience of coping with their own process and the respect that goes with this. If we are in a position to help, we do so only if asked and only if it actually helps without disempowering them.

If, instead, we take on their pain or grief, or if we try to fix them because we can't bear their suffering, it usually indicates we have not dealt with some similar painful events in our own lives. When we have resolved the issues surrounding our wounds and learned how to deal with the pain—experiencing it without resistance and then letting it go—we gain understanding, patience and compassion. Sometimes this has meant seeking out more effective, proactive ways of coping, or standing up to injustice where it can make a difference. When there is nothing we can do to change a situation, we simply need to accept it. Sometimes, we need to forgive others and ourselves, and simply let it go.

Whatever the painful process, taking responsibility for resolving our own problems might mean that we sometimes forego approval or even support from a meaningful other, but this results in better skills, greater resilience and confidence, and a deeper sense of our Selves. Why would we deny ourselves, or someone we love, this valuable opportunity to grow as a person?

Chapter 20

Interdependence

In good relationships we can be independent and *inter*dependent—which means we learn how to find or give ourselves what we need as adults, rather than depending on our partner to make us feel secure or happy, or tell us what we should do. At the same time, we value the synergy of being with someone we love and who loves us. We learn how to give and take. We make ourselves into the kind of friend we would like to have, without demanding this from others. We find good friends, a loyal lover and fulfilling work relationships. As adults, our relationships with our parents, family members and others can be equal, not needy or controlling, or overly responsible or accommodating. And with these friends, relatives, lovers and work colleagues, we can create relationships with each that provide us with fun, excitement, satisfaction and benefit for all involved.

Most of the time we show only part of ourselves to others. In turn they may only perceive parts of us, though not necessarily the same parts we think we're showing. Often there's a whole range of people with whom we do not care to share all of our lives: we need to keep something in ourselves hidden from others, until we are sure of how to approach it. There's nothing wrong with this, in itself. We need to discern whether we are sharing as much as we want to share in all our relationships, or whether we are falling into a dysfunctional pattern that we might have had with less than ideal parents.

However, when we enjoy a full relationship, a loving marriage or a family relationship, we're then able to interact openly and wholeheartedly with any person we might meet.

Individuals are as rich and varied as universes. My universe comprises my body, health, thoughts, feelings and desires, as well as my inner, spiritual life and my growth path as an individual and as a professional in my career. In it are also representations of the family I grew up with, and perhaps my recreational activities. I learn responsibility by experiencing the consequences of my actions. I learn to handle both loneliness and being alone, which are not the same thing. I find ways to entertain myself, organize my time, and deal with problems and obstacles. As a result I become strong, resourceful, creative and *interesting*. If my life on my own is not rich, happy, satisfyingly challenging and interesting to me, it's unlikely that it will attract others with those qualities. It's a complete system—up to a point. An old teacher of mine used to say we can never really live with another human being in full interdependence until we have learned to live, happily, entirely alone. And when we can do that, that's when we realize that there are things we can learn only from sharing our life with another person.

The magical other I attract has his own rich universe. The only time I should be involved with this *second universe* is by invitation. And then, it is not my business to advise unless asked, or to interfere. The main job of a partner is to listen and to empathize, to understand and not to judge or criticize, to support with true help that does not lessen in any way the individuality or the independence of the other. And along with this experience are love, respect, admiration, fun and pure joy.

When my partner and I are together, there is a *third universe* of our relationship. We create it with the chemistry of our attraction/interaction in the present moment and when we think of each other, or do things for each other when we are apart.

The third universe of our relationship is a space that we consciously create in much the same way that we create ourselves—with intentions, aspirations, new experiences, memories and growth paths. It's a living thing, buzzing with contentment and enjoyment, alive with possibilities and harmonious connections.

We actively love and appreciate our partner in the same way and sexual chemistry between us makes our time together unpredictable and exciting. Shared values and mutual respect create a firm foundation for a family or long-term partnership. Ideally, we each contribute to the third universe by bringing our whole selves into it. It starts with just being who we are and expands with the synergy of our shared creativity. It allows us to reach out to the other at will. Equally, it allows us at times to withdraw to a more private internal space, without strings to the universe of the relationship.

Sometimes we may give or receive more, as will our partner. This ebb and flow is a natural, sustainable aspect of a good relationship, indicating a trusting, supportive partnership between differentiated individuals. The joint space that we enter makes being together pleasant, productive and at best, magical and full of passion. It means we don't need a cord between us to feel connected. We can simply look at each other to create a harmonic connection, or tune in and know what the other is feeling, and be able to communicate openly and fully about that. The space that we create together is our own harmonious third universe.

For this to happen it's essential to create our own personal universe where we have a nourishing space for rest and recreation and where we can be happily on our own. If we do not do this—and in an ongoing way—the third universe gradually becomes a way we prefer to define ourselves. If our personal, primary universe is not healthy or happy, we might draw too heavily on the third universe. We might equally fight what has become its suffocating energy to us.

If we are undifferentiated in a relationship, we cannot be ourselves. We might fight for independence by hiding parts of ourselves, usually for protection or to keep some part unshared. When either partner is hiding their true selves, they are more likely to rely on an energetic connection such as a cord that allows secret access to how their partner is thinking or feeling. We become dependent or co-dependent, and our connection becomes a toxic cord relationship.

This doesn't mean we should be completely open in sharing with our partner every single little thing that is happening for us. Some things are irrelevant to the relationship—say, in the details of our work or professional life. Be careful, though, if you find yourself keeping anything secret from your partner, or if there is anything in your daily life you would prefer your partner not to know. It's actually a level of cheating by closing off a part of ourselves. The shame we feel in hiding things from our partner means we guiltily stop ourselves from being open with them in other ways. It sows suspicion and doubt. Without knowing exactly what we are withholding, our partner will feel on some level shut out.

If on the other hand we can keep differentiated boundaries, it means we allow a free and open flow of energy that belongs to the relationship. There is nothing hidden. We can communicate what we are feeling and thinking as appropriate, without the defensive barriers that result in dumping or feeling insecure.

Have a look at your most important relationship. How would you describe it? Can you share your space openheartedly or do you hold something back? Just for reference, consider your parents' partnership. Is there any similarity? Looking back at your own central relationship, your third universe, consider what might make it a richer, nourishing, creative space for each of you to grow to be more passionately your real Selves.

Chapter 21

How does a connection turn toxic?

A cord that starts full of love and nurturing can become toxic without either person being aware of what is happening. It often begins when one of them comes to believe the other's opinion of them matters more than their own. In other words, when they lose self-differentiation, or perhaps never had it in the first place. Their behavior and attitudes are determined by the other's dictates, either in compliance or rebellion, or to placate.

Cords are often used to control another person—especially children—under the guise of caring, but really coming from neediness or from fear of loss. We don't need cords to love our children, to guide and use appropriate discipline to help them become decent and considerate individuals. To achieve a cord-free relationship means we need to reach a deeper level of love in our caring, where we can provide a platform for our kids to become increasingly emotionally responsible and self-determined as they grow. In this way we also model how they can be.

If we have grown up enmeshed with our own parents in cord relationships, to be cord-free is extremely difficult to achieve in adult life. Any time we're stressed, say in a typical sleep-deprived or care-burdened parental moment, we might revert to the less than ideal behavior that our own parents modeled for us. It happens even if we are appalled at what we are doing and vowed never to do this.

HOW CAN I AVOID REPEATING
MY PARENTS' MISTAKES?

It's a long process, but we can begin to break the pattern by first learning from our parents' deficiencies what not to do. It takes calm reflection and detachment to allow more conscious, effective behavior. We need to see what causes the core emotions of fear and anger that are at the bottom of anxiety or overcontrol. Basically, we need to gain some perspective. How would we do it differently? What is stopping us? What stopped our parents? Have we forgiven them? Forgiveness is crucial here because of a paradox: our resistance to becoming like them can bring that very thing about. Forgiveness doesn't mean we forget, however, and in most cases it's important not to forget what has been such a powerful lesson.

As adolescents we find it too easy to blame our parents for their inadequacies and mistakes. We can use the cord then to punish them. If power has been wielded this way by our parents, even unconsciously, we know exactly how to abuse it ourselves to exact our revenge and assert our own power. It's particularly effective by remote control with behavior that disappoints and worries them. Before long, we are lost in a tangle of cord toxicity.

Being so defined by such relationships to parents or others means we lose our sense of Self. It's an unpleasant situation where we feel we are fighting in close confines for space and freedom, while being controlled by something we can't quite put our finger on.

Then, of course, because we're not our own person, we're primed to fall in love with Prince Charming or Snow White, or whoever looks close enough to serve for our projection. We idealize the person we meet and create a third universe that is really a fantasy of idealized love into which we can escape from our parental dungeon or imprisoning tower. It's an illusion, and the truth is there will be no "happy ever after."

This fantasy universe is at first energetically separate from our own personal universe, full of fairy tales and unrealistic romantic scenarios as opposed to a solid third universe created with truth and reciprocal nurturing.

Also, if our personal universe is full of secret, shameful negative thoughts and painful, angry emotions, a fantasy perfect romance is exactly what we might use to try to replace it. The problem is, we can sometimes lose ourselves in it.

For a time the fantasy third universe we are creating with our lover has nothing of the discomfort we experience in our personal space. In it, we are in bliss, excited, joy-filled, at peace and optimistic, perfectly content. We create this third universe continuously whenever we're together. We fill it with hopes and dreams when apart. We withhold from it any negativity, including any self-hatred or low self-esteem we might secretly harbor. Instinctively we don't want to contaminate this perfect shared space with any of our less-than-perfect past history. The difference between our personal universe and the fantasy romance universe becomes extreme. For a time, perhaps a few weeks or months, it's sustainable, but when we leave the romance universe and go back to being on our own, all our former demons return.

It is then we might rely on the fantasy third universe for respite, to displace our discomfort. Drawing on it energetically, it stretches to become a pipeline. Then we begin to off-load into it some of our nastier energy. It's not a conscious thing. We're simply treating it like the cords we've always had in previous relationships in which we were not completely our own person.

Now the cord between us fills with all the stuff we don't want. Irritation, unspoken expectations and disappointments, fear and grasping need, resentment and sadness begin to flow backward and forward through the cord. Some of this stuff doesn't even belong to the current relationship but is triggered by it. By this stage the once distinct and separate third universe has morphed into a fully toxic cord, where we no longer know who we are in the relationship. Even after we've split, the cord remains active, along with all the older toxic cords.

Chapter 22

The curious effect of clearing toxic attachments

When people have been entangled in a cord relationship for long enough to feel restricted or exploited, what happens after the cord is cleared is often dramatic—a spectacular change in how they feel about themselves, their lives and the other person.

It's common for people to feel freer to do things they've always wanted to do, but not allowed themselves to do before. Becoming free of a cloying or destructive relationship sometimes allows even physical results such as a sudden growth spurt in an adolescent, or renewed passion in a long-married couple's love life. Often clearing one cord has a clarifying effect on any other cords that are based on the same kind of dynamic.

THE FREEDOM OF DISENTANGLEMENT

Twenty-six-year-old Samantha had felt compelled by financial needs to stay in a job she hated. She was bound by the echo of her mother's voice telling her she couldn't have everything she wanted in life and that everyone had to do things they didn't enjoy. When we looked at what was going on for Samantha, she realized this attitude wasn't just coming from her mother. Samantha saw a cord that went back through generations of women. In her traditionally matriarchal family this cord controlled how she dressed, thought and behaved, and of course to whom and when she "should" be married.

After clearing this cord Samantha started her own business, something she had believed would forever remain a fantasy. She began to experiment with her clothes and try different "looks" she'd been too uncertain to try before. She did some things she'd never allowed herself to do—like taking a vacation on her own. To her astonishment, she was now able to laugh off her mother's pessimistic predictions and not take them on board. Some time after this she noticed her mother was no longer voicing her negativity—at least while Samantha was around.

SIBLINGS

Cords between adult siblings can be extraordinarily toxic, full of jealousy that is often a legacy of an imbalance of parental approval in childhood, whether real or imagined. It's common that one child of the family, the "black sheep," becomes the accepted scapegoat for

175

any family troubles, and the subject of family conversations full of disapproving eye rolls and exasperated head shaking by other more favored members of the family. Sibling rivalry can manifest in ongoing competitions of perceived material success, prestige, achievements, a fortunate marriage, sometimes even the number of offspring and their successes. The list is probably endless. Clearing a cord between adult siblings can bring peace and acceptance and the affection of real sisterhood and brotherhood that may never have existed in childhood. If not this ideal outcome, a clearing allows a parting of the ways without strings of blame or resentment.

TWINS

A cord between twins—whether identical or not—is usually more apparent than between other siblings. In documented cases where separated twins go to different adoptive parents and are not told anything of their birth family, a persistent feeling of incompleteness will sometimes motivate a search in which one turns up the other twin. Often the similarities in their lives are eerie, even to the names of their spouses or their children. The cord that formed between them as they shared a womb allows this unknown resonance, and it's the cord that reunites them.

In twins brought up together, the risk of toxicity in a cord becomes greater if their parents—or the twins themselves—have not fostered individuality in everything from their clothes to their hobbies. When your twin has shared everything in your life, even small differences are significant. Even so, the temptation to form a "secret society" of twinhood, sometimes with its own language and code, can be both a delicious alliance against the rest of the world and simultaneously make a prison of closeness. A clearing of the cords between twins often means each one can mature in ways that may have been restricted. Like thin and weedy seedlings that have outgrown a small basket, each twin can find space to spread their roots and grow strong, though separate.

MY BROTHER'S KEEPER

Magnus and his brother Jude were "Irish" twins—born on the same day exactly a year apart. They enjoyed the fact they looked so similar people often mistook them for twins.

At 18, Magnus developed a severe condition that required a kidney transplant. Jude didn't hesitate to offer one of his kidneys to his younger brother and the operations went ahead without a hitch. After a few months, however, there was an inexplicable reversal and Magnus died. The shock to Jude was immense. He felt half of him had died. Even worse, just as Jude felt he was emerging from the long grieving period, he began to develop some of the same symptoms his brother had prior to his diagnosis. Jude, however, now had only one kidney and the situation was worrying.

Jude had been doing grief therapy, working on letting go of an irrational guilt he still carried despite having done everything he could to help Magnus. It was in this period that he realized he still had a cord to his brother, and that from their infancy he had always felt he was responsible for Magnus. Even though Magnus was dead, Jude felt he was somehow carrying him. Believing that he had failed to help his brother, he was energetically taking on his illness as a way of punishing himself.

When we cleared the cord, Jude's symptoms stopped. He reported in the following days that he was sure Magnus had come to visit him one night in spirit, and it had been with the kind of affectionate brotherly kidding around they had always shared. Jude said that though he would always miss his brother, he now felt free to lead his own life with greater appreciation and joy.

A LEGACY OF SYMPTOMS

In my work I've come across many clients who develop similar symptoms to deceased loved ones soon after their death, even though they have shown none of those signs beforehand. In most cases it's because of the energetic and emotional content that makes up the bulk of the cord. Usually that content is guilt, whether warranted or not. In many cases, guilt originates in the deceased at some wrong they have done to the other person. It then resonates with the energy of the survivor on the other end of the cord.

This happened with Callie, whose father had been distant during her childhood and estranged from the entire family since her teenage years. Years later, he was diagnosed with an aggressive cancer and before he died, he contacted Callie's family asking that they come to his deathbed. His request was a shock that took some time for Callie to assimilate. Unfortunately, her father died just hours before she got to the hospice. It was the first time she had seen him in nearly 20 years. At his funeral, she was amazed at the depth of the grief she felt, as well as the overwhelming guilt.

Within two months, Callie was showing disturbing symptoms similar to her father's, and tests revealed cysts that might be cancerous.

In the period of exploration of the cord before it was cleared, and while Callie was having biopsies, she managed to make a distinction between the 10 percent of her own guilt and the other 90 percent coming to her in a cord from her father. Before the clearing process, Callie forgave her father, and forgave herself for not letting go of her resentment sooner. In less than a fortnight the cysts disappeared completely. Meanwhile the biopsies she'd had done before this showed the cysts were benign. Callie is certain the guilt she was receiving in the cord manifested as cysts in her body, though in her father's body the guilt had become malignant tumors.

Chapter 23

Positive reconnections

Sometimes cord clearings can achieve reconnections. As the toxic content of an old cord is recognized and then cleared, the Higher Self connection between two people can reassert itself. As well as helping to mend family and love relationships gone wrong, a cord clearing can restore friendships when things have gotten out of whack, as happened in Jennifer and Heidi's story.

Jennifer and Heidi had been best friends from elementary school. Now in their 30s, openhearted, sunny-natured Jennifer was married with two kids, while Heidi was a competitive career woman with a long trail of damaging partnerships and no kids.

In one liaison, Heidi would be the Rescuer, caring for and helping her lover. In the next, she would be the Victim of a controlling or violent man. She seemed unable to change these alternating roles. Jennifer's heart ached for her friend. She knew she was the only one that Heidi confided in about her most painful secrets and her fears. With the pride of the Rescuer, Heidi was unable to admit she was suffering after her latest breakup. In her eyes it would mean she was weak and pathetic, as she had been all through her abusive childhood. Then and now, Jennifer was her only ally.

The cord between them had always functioned more in Heidi's favor, at least on the surface. Tenderhearted Jennifer was very aware that she took Heidi's pain on board, often crying long into the night after a lengthy personal conversation. Heidi, on the other hand, simply put on her Happy Face Character and felt fine, until her growing discomfort—manifesting as blocked sinuses, headaches and cramps—indicated she needed another off-loading session with her best friend.

Having worked with me before, Jennifer came to the session aware there was a cord and wanting to clear it. She felt she had reached the saturation point. She acknowledged that she was also inadvertently making things worse for Heidi, because in taking on her pain she was preventing her friend from learning the lessons of her disastrous hookups as well as how to handle the fallout. Jennifer realized that in Heidi's attempt to suppress her distress, she had blocked all other outlets of expression. When Heidi confided in Jennifer she let everything out in a torrent, without reflecting on any of it. It meant she never got perspective on her situation to learn from it. Heidi openly denied that she was really hurt much of the time, and it had gotten to the point that she needed Jennifer's empathic reactions to identify how she was feeling underneath. In return, Jennifer's own sadness and sympathy for her friend was recycled back into the cord to Heidi, making Heidi even less resourceful.

Jennifer was torn between wanting to be there for her friend, being a better mom for her than her own mother had been, and wanting to say that she was no longer willing to be her dumpster. Too kind to actually say anything, she had the cord cleared.

The effect of the clearing astonished her.

Heidi's next call to her was far from the usual needy litany of disasters. It was to tell Jennifer she had started going to counseling. The flow of heavy toxic muck she usually dumped on her friend stopped. As Heidi learned to take responsibility for herself, their friendship grew stronger than ever. It became even better when Heidi had the cord with her mother cleared. A little while later—for the first time in her life—Heidi found herself in a relationship with a different kind of man, one who was considerate and appreciative of her best qualities. And Jennifer is enjoying a much more equal, reciprocal friendship with her best friend.

In follow-up sessions two weeks after a clearing, to ensure everything has gone well and that the cord is gone, my clients answer a questionnaire. Typical comments include: "I feel so much more like myself." "I hardly think of X now, and when I do I don't get sucked into the old misery and regret."

People often comment that they can see the positive traits of the person they formerly had antipathy toward; that they are less emotionally reactive and able to be assertive and to communicate honestly. Often people feel detached, not concerned with what the other person thinks anymore, or they are able to let the other person, with whom they had a codependent relationship, handle their own problems and not rush in to fix them anymore. And one client commented that she'd stopped writing her "misery memoir" since she didn't need to anymore. She felt she'd moved on and was so much happier. The comment most often made after a clearing is that people have a lot more energy, feel healthier and more balanced all-around.

Chapter 24

Using relationships to evolve

The first time we fall in love we might believe it is forever, only to have our heart broken. We might avoid relationships for quite some time thereafter, hoping never to be hurt again. Of course, it's likely we will fall in love once more. But if we approach a new love affair with fear that it will fail like the last, we might subconsciously create exactly the same dynamic.

How can we learn from our mistakes so we don't repeat them? When we think of these mistakes, we can be flooded by emotion. These are the times we knew beforehand someone was wrong for us but allowed ourselves to fall in love anyway. There was the warning from a close friend about a straying lover that we ignored, maybe even blaming the messenger and losing a good friend. Or the times we chose to ignore the feeling that our lover was lying to us. We might have believed what both of us wanted to believe about the other, only to find ourselves disillusioned when we discover the self-deception on both sides. Or we might have been blindsided, trusting someone about whom we had no clue, who then heartlessly betrayed us. Whatever we feel when we remember these heart-wrenching breakups, the main emotion comes down to fear that we will be betrayed by our own lack of perception about character or by a callous liar, that we will be hurt again.

But fear blinds us to what we need to know. Wherever you got in your partnership before it broke up, take some time, calm the fear and have a look at the times in the relationship you knew there was something wrong. What was it that let you know? Was it some incongruence between what your lover said and did? Was it that promises were never followed by action? Was it the feeling that he or she was mentally somewhere else, not there with you? One client told me she knew her husband was cheating on her because his lovemaking style had changed. She felt it was someone else's likes and dislikes he was responding to, and not hers. Another told me she knew her new lover was not really with her, because it was obvious he was kissing her automatically, as he used to kiss his ex-wife. She could see he simply wasn't in the present moment.

It's important we're aware of the traps we fell into previously and know that next time we can avoid them. It helps when we have the attitude that each relationship is unique even when there are similarities, so we have a chance at not repeating mistakes. It's like starting a new day on which we can create something different from yesterday, something better. A second chance. Or a third.

There's a saying that hindsight is always 20/20. When we use these valuable insights, they can give us an enormous amount of information to create better relationships and better lives in our future—particularly about what not to do. But if old cords are influencing how we are relating, we might feel that nothing we can do will make a difference in a new relationship.

The first step to healing the wound of a difficult or painful relationship is detachment. However, before we can fully detach from the cords with parents, siblings, friends and partners that keep us stuck, we need to become aware that we have them. As you reflect on past relationships—can you see repeated patterns?

This is where a skilled therapist can help greatly. If our new partnership also has problems, we can either address those issues with more confidence, or end the relationship sooner rather than later, without too much pain. We can move on more easily. As a result, the next relationship, or the one after that, will be far closer to our ideal.

In fact, what happens is that we are using romantic relationships in a positive way to evolve as a person. Not only are we discovering what we want and need, we also discover aspects of our own personality that need changing—and are able to implement those changes proactively instead of running for protection. It's through reflecting on our patterns of behavior that we can see the evolution process at work. If in the past we have been attracted only to damaged, manipulative people, we now begin to be attracted to partners who are healthier, who come close to our ideal. And these healthier people are attracted in their turn.

FAILURE TO LAUNCH

At 38, Bradley still lived at home, justifying his failure to launch with the good excuse of having to look after his mother, Miriam, after his father died five years before. In truth, he was afraid of moving out and too comfortable having his washing done, his meals cooked and his role defined, even in such a limiting way. At the same time he complained of being treated like a child and, ignoring his own recalcitrance, blamed Miriam for not letting him have a life of his own.

Spitefully, he would attempt to transfer his affection to the occasional date. His mother, equally afraid of being alone, fussed over him while complaining about his irritability, stubbornness and lack of communication about where he was going when he went out. Essentially, it had been this way between them all Bradley's life.

At this stage, his attempted romantic relationships never developed past the first date. Most of the women he met noticed the Mommy's Boy Character straightaway. Some became aware also of the covert spite he employed to distance himself from his mother. For her part, Miriam felt him pulling away from her and the anxiety and displeasure this caused her was injected into the cord. Unable to differentiate his mother's emotion from his own, and to avoid being hurt, Bradley would find fault with the woman, criticize her harshly, and that would be the end of it.

Not being able to distance himself from his mother's emotions, Bradley had developed a narcissistic focus on his own needs and was unable to empathize with others. Miriam felt his anger. It fed her fear of being abandoned and her resentment at being unappreciated and exploited. In denying and suppressing these unpleasant emotions, she transmitted them to Bradley, and so the vicious cycle went on. On one level Miriam was very familiar with this situation. She had had much the same relationship with her mother.

It didn't change until Miriam was coaxed by a friend to join her in learning tai chi. As she practiced this ancient Chinese gentle martial art form, she released toxic energy from her body. It brought new awareness of the life force—chi—flowing in her body as well as a new concept of freedom. When offered a chance to go with the group on a tai chi tour of China, she took it. Away for nearly six weeks, her attention was on the many amazing, unfamiliar sights she was seeing for the first time. The cycle of toxic emotions in the cord began to break down.

When Miriam returned, feeling freer than she had ever felt, this flowed through the cord to Bradley. Not long after, he met a woman on a dating Web site and began a deeper relationship with her than he'd ever had. In turn, Miriam began seeing a man from her tai chi class. Bradley then announced he was moving out to live with his girlfriend in her house. Buoyed up by the positive changes she felt within herself, Miriam agreed it was time.

For some months after moving out Bradley continued to call his mother twice a day, to his partner's annoyance. Miriam and Bradley were now playing a more solicitous role over the other's welfare, but it was more mechanical than helpful. Each of them tended to ignore the advice the other gave.

As Miriam continued to work on herself—through tai chi and later through meditation, yoga, therapy and cord clearing—their relationship evolved from destructive to accepting, supportive and nourishing.

A PATTERN OF BETRAYAL

Evan's first marriage was an unhappy mistake that lasted only a year. His second was completely different, and for 15 years he believed he was happy. There were a few things that rankled him but he ignored them, preferring to "look on the bright side" as he had been taught as a child. When he discovered his wife was secretly filing for divorce and planning to leave him for a younger man, he reeled in disbelief. He began to look at his supposedly satisfactory life more closely.

In therapy he uncovered old wounds that had influenced many of his choices. It became apparent that betrayal was a common theme in his life. His father had left his mother penniless when Evan was five and his sister only two. A great deal of pressure had been put on him to "be the man of the house." At the time, Evan identified so closely with his mother that he felt his father's desertion as a personal betrayal. Then when he was 12, he felt his mother betrayed him by marrying again.

His own first marriage was the choice of his Rescuer Character and failed due to his wife's compulsive infidelity from the wedding day onward. His second marriage was ostensibly based on equality. His new wife had a façade of an astute businesswoman with no need for protection or rescue. In reality, she was badly damaged from childhood abuse and the Positive Thinker/Career Woman Character that she projected covered deep insecurities.

Through exploring the cord he had with his second wife, Evan recognized in hindsight that he felt in her the same grasping neediness he had felt from his mother through the early years, and the same insecurity as with his first wife.

After his second divorce Evan embarked on a series of brief, uncommitted relationships. These affairs proved to be variations on the, by now familiar, theme of betrayal. The fact that people were continuing to betray him indicated he was somehow attracting the same kind of person. Could it be that he was making choices of partners who would let him down?

Evan began to look at how this dynamic might be operating in his life. His childhood wounds meant he had unconsciously chosen women with lower self-esteem than his own. All had camouflaged their insecurity to varying degrees, just as his mother had. He began to see more deeply into their personalities instead of simply accepting them at face value. He saw that because they rated themselves as less worthy than him, they would never dare challenge him to face his own feared deficiencies. Instead, they protected him from seeing his own faults, in exchange for his protection. At the same time, they resented their own neediness.

Evan realized his Rescuer was still very much running his life, spotlighting others' needs at the expense of his own, giving him a false sense of pride and superiority. The cord with his mother was where this pattern had begun. When in the course of time the cord they shared was cleared, Evan said he felt like a new man, free for the first time to be truly himself. He is currently in a close relationship with the healthiest and least insecure person he has ever known. She challenges him to face and conquer his own fear in ways he has never allowed himself to do before.

Chapter 25

Is my soul mate out there?

There is a popular belief that love is forever and there is one Ms. or Mr. Right out there for everyone. Included in this idea is that almost every love story ends in "Happily Ever After." It's good to remember that these are fairy tales.

There's a raft of illusions that love should be effortless, that we match our partner perfectly, that our partner should be able to read our mind without our needing to say anything, that sexual chemistry means true love, that love means never having to say we're sorry and other complete fallacies.

The real story is that as individuals we will often clash with others. We will have different likes and dislikes, aims and goals. It's not a bad thing. It just presents another challenge for us to communicate authentically, effectively and with mutual respect.

The value of relationships is not simply to keep us feeling safe, comfortable and happy; it's when we find someone with whom we can grow to be more our true selves in a way we cannot when we are single.

If our relationship is important to us, it necessarily means that consideration, negotiation and change are all part of the deal. This is almost impossible to achieve when there are toxic cords that drain energy from the partnership, or because cord-related patterns of behavior from old relationships stop the individuals from growing.

Let's try the following variation on the fairy-tale ending, one that looks for a more evolved and realistic, but still an ideal, relationship. It's an approach that uses our past relationships to evolve into better current ones.

A good, potentially lasting relationship allows enough similarity to feel comfortable and enough difference to feel interested, challenged and stimulated by being together. It's important we *share the same values*, including how we feel about money, friends, different cultures, ambition, health, education and children. It's better to have *similar belief systems* or to at least respect the other's beliefs. It sounds almost too basic that we should *like each other*, and yet many a married couple in trouble will admit that they don't really like each other, despite love or sexual attraction. It's also important that we *find each other attractive and sexy*; we *enjoy each other's thought processes*; we find *each other funny* and *like each other's smell, look and body shape*. It's especially important that we *admire and respect each other* and that we are equally matched in the ability to be *intimate, physically affectionate, caring and considerate*.

On top of these basic requirements are the need for excellent communication skills, including empathy, assertiveness and sincerity; the ability to take responsibility for our own emotional state and comfort ourselves—in other words, to be equally emotionally mature. We need to be able to discuss anything calmly, with nothing we can't talk about; a willingness to admit we are wrong and to learn from our mistakes; an ability to seek the best possible solution for all parties to any problem or conflict that might arise. We have no secrets from each other.

I find many people who come to me for couples counseling are lacking in the fundamentals for a good relationship, let alone communications skills or other personal qualities that enable good sharing. It's not that they deliberately chose the wrong person or want to be miserable. They simply chose their partner for other reasons than the viability of the relationship: from need or fear of being alone, to escape another situation, on sexual chemistry or on the basis of a fantasy they have projected onto their partner. Much of the disappointment people experience in a relationship comes from a partner not fulfilling their fantasy. Disappointment indicates our expectations were unrealistic—unless we have been deceived by false promises.

So how does this work? Let's say we've learned from mistakes in previous relationships. We now know there are some things in a partnership that are important for us to share, some that are essential and others that are not. We've figured out what is important to us, what we need to give and to receive. Then, we find our wonderful mate and have the ideal basis for a relationship—we like each other, share similar backgrounds, values and beliefs, and we can communicate easily and well.

We create a magical, thrilling third universe. In this space we can talk about anything at all and nothing is off the table. We have good communication skills. We love and admire each other. Better still, we like each other, even at odd times when we don't feel especially in love. We find the other sexy and fun, we like their sense of humor. We like to do many of the same things together and we are also happy to pursue interests on our own, sharing the later telling of it. We are more or less equally healthy, equally financially secure and equally independent adults.

Yet even with this ideal, each of us brings baggage to the relationship. We cannot avoid this. Why? Because we've been conditioned by previous relationships into certain ways of relating. We've been hurt, betrayed and deluded, which makes us wary and perhaps less open than the first time we fell in love. Or, for some second-timers, we've had one long, loving relationship end by the death of the spouse. The expectations and assumptions that arise here can be equally problematic in a new relationship. There will likely be a toxic cord or two from our past partners we were not aware of, which become active in close interactions with our new partner.

How can we avoid the past spoiling the present? Unless we can be in the here and now in the relationship, we will allow past toxic cords to influence us. We'll then form new cords with our new partner similar to those that already bind us. Being in the present allows us to see where the emotion we are feeling is coming from: is it the current situation or is it triggered by something in the past? Is it our emotion or does it come from someone else?

Then we need to communicate honestly, so the current relationship can grow in trust and deeper love. Initially, we might not even see that we're caught in certain emotional patterns. It's the water we are swimming in and often we can't see the currents.

Even in an ideal relationship, problems and conflicts will arise. It's how we deal with them that indicates the health and longevity of our relationship.

Chapter 26

What hope have I got with parents like mine?

Sometimes, anything or anyone seems preferable to life with our parents. Kelly fled home at 19, for a marriage that she believed would save her from her dysfunctional relationships with her psychotic mother and her philandering father. Instead, her husband turned out to be the worst combination of both parents, an exploitive, manipulating adulterer. Through the birth and raising of her three children, Kelly weathered it out, believing it must be her fault that she was so unhappy. That's what her husband frequently told her. Escaping the marriage as soon as she could, and still young at 38, she embarked on a succession of dead-end relationships that lasted at most a few years at a time.

When our cords with our parents are strong we are vulnerable. We're unconsciously attracted to a similar energy or relationship. It can make us feel that there are no other options in how to relate or that the only way out is to flee anything that reminds us of our powerlessness. And it's then that we end up marrying our fathers or our mothers.

Seeing that the partners we have chosen have been wrong for us does not necessarily mean we're sabotaging ourselves. Each partnership is an opportunity for us to work out and perhaps resolve our parental issues in an arena that doesn't have the same mucky history. Observing that we are behaving with a new partner in similar dysfunctional ways as we did with an old partner, or with our parents, is a huge awakening. It's a sure indication that a cord has been operating below our awareness until now. The secret is to have more detachment when the same issues start to appear.

Nevertheless, it is easier to work these issues out with someone new. They can teach us things the old relationship could not. Through therapy Kelly was learning bit by bit to handle and overcome repeating patterns of her childhood. She became aware that each relationship was an echo of a different aspect of the cords she had with her parents. She had been too entangled in cords with her parents to unravel her Self while living with them.

Her first marriage had been a disaster because it mirrored too closely the enmeshment with her parents. In her later partnerships she felt she had more space, and while she still battled with the illusion of "Happily Ever After," she realized each relationship, while far from ideal, was teaching her something precious. She was learning what it was she needed emotionally, what she found meaningful and what unimportant, how she wanted to communicate and share intimately, how deeply she wanted to love someone who could match her equally.

Once she learned the particular lesson of each relationship, she could differentiate herself, and move on, better informed, more mature and more self-determined. These gifts also enabled her to cope more easily with the emotional pain of ending relationships that could go no further.

When Kelly reflected on her development, she commented that each new relationship was with a man who seemed to be the very opposite to her last one. One would adore her, but have no spine or initiative. The next would appear to be wise, but would bully and dominate her. The one after that was spontaneous and playful, but unreliable. And so on. Through going from one extreme to another, she was trying to find balance in how to relate. Finally, through much introspection and work in therapy, Kelly realized that these choices were not self-sabotage and she could stop blaming herself and feeling bad. She was on her own side.

Clearing cords one by one as she retraced her connections, Kelly gradually became freer of their entangling energy. She became more differentiated, more empowered and wiser in choosing a partner.

It struck Kelly at last that each of her past relationships mirrored evolving stages of her personal growth. She knew she was becoming wiser, more resilient and better able to assert herself. She was evolving into a more complete person, and though it was still important to her to find a good, lasting relationship, she was no longer relying on a partner to save her or to make her happy. She was finding out how to create happiness for herself. This led to a confident hope that when she had reached a certain point of maturity, she would find her perfect mate. And that is exactly what she attracted.

Even in this wonderful relationship, Kelly is challenged to remain in the present, to not fall into automatic ways of behaving, to communicate as honestly as she can and to take responsibility for her emotions—especially when she recognizes her samskaric wounds are being triggered. She feels there's a good chance the relationship will last this time because both of them are working equally toward making the relationship work. When both partners are present and honest in their communicating, their intimacy deepens, and so the love they share and the joy they find in each other continues to grow.

Chapter 27

Learning to trust our own judgment

Fear of betraying ourselves with our own illusions about who the people we love are can paralyze us. How can we know whether to trust them? How can we know whether to trust ourselves?

Think about this. If you knew someone was a thief, you wouldn't leave your wallet lying around. You'd trust them to be a thief. Similarly if you knew someone to be a heartbreaker, you wouldn't leave your heart around to be walked on or torn into pieces. You'd trust them to be a heartbreaker. But here you are really trusting yourself—your own knowledge and judgment.

Learning who to trust and for what, and who not to believe, begins with knowing ourselves. Learning about ourselves, we can then communicate honestly and openly, even when we're afraid. We can own our fear and open our hearts anyway, even if it's little by little. It takes courage, but it gets easier. If we're not deluding ourselves, if we know ourselves, we can also soothe ourselves when we're hurt. We can talk about it and sort it out instead of running and hiding.

We need to be differentiated human beings, able to connect with others and also to detach when we need to—say at work in an everyday sense, but also when a relationship has reached a natural end.

Detachment means no longer allowing your emotional center to be tied to another person. You can be yourself without worrying what people think of you, and what they do no longer worries or upsets you. This is not about being selfish in a self-absorbed sort of way, but about looking after your own emotional needs and by being responsible for your own emotional state. Only you allow yourself to be affected by someone else, and while that's human, it becomes unhealthy when we cannot regain balance and soothe ourselves when we're hurt or upset.

An unhealthy relationship might be too clingy, needy, manipulative, exploitive, bullying or rejecting. Detaching from something like that when we've been tangled up in it takes courage. We have to become more resilient, more self-sufficient. This in turn means we can connect more deeply and lovingly the next time, with an open heart.

The more we communicate, the more we get to know and understand someone. The more we understand, the more there is to like or love. The more we like them, the more we communicate in trust and love. It's a virtuous circle.

On the other hand, the more we withhold from communication, the less we know a person and the less they know us and the more confusion we allow in our relationship. The more confusion and uncertainty—the more fear and anxiety—the less trust and affinity. The more anxiety there is, the less communication—a vicious circle.

So we have a choice. It all really depends on whether we let fear rule us, or love—the giddy uncertainty of illusion and fantasy, or the far more exciting journey of understanding ourselves and the people we love.

Chapter 28

When the going gets tough

In any long-term relationship, it's likely that at some stage the partners have experienced some sort of threatening crisis—a tragedy, an illness or an unexpected challenge that results in a temporary breakup or separation. Perhaps one partner has an extramarital affair or there's a time when the individuals are growing in different directions. Both of you might think the marriage is over. In cases where you have grown apart, it will be.

There are no guarantees in any relationship, but one that is not based on cords has more chance of surviving hardship than one that is bound by them.

So what happens when one partner is going through a bad time—is the pain shared, halved or doubled? When 48-year-old Rick went to the hospital after an accident, his wife, Alicia, at first rarely left his side. Rick soon realized that when Alicia came into the room, his stress level increased and his pain became unbearable. His pain levels improved and he relaxed when Alicia was not there.

When he began to dread visiting hours, he asked the nursing staff to tell his wife when she came that he was asleep, so he could rest. When he came home, his pain medication dosage tripled until he told Alicia that he found it difficult to get better when she was constantly there attending to him.

This is not an uncommon situation. In pain experiments described by physiotherapist David Butler, patients with a caring, attentive partner experienced more pain than those with an uncaring spouse.[23]

Alicia was bewildered and hurt. She had taken time off work to nurse Rick through his recuperation and felt she was expressing her love for him in the best way she knew. As she explained to me, when *she* was ill or injured, she felt it helped her get better when there was at least one person constantly there looking after her. It was the way her own mother had looked after her as a child.

I asked Rick how he felt when Alicia was tending to him. He said his pain grew much worse when he saw her worried about him and when she seemed to be suffering from the added stress his bedridden condition was causing her, especially financially. Then I asked him how he felt when she was ill. Pressured, he said. He found her constant neediness intolerable. Anyway, he told her, why couldn't she just let herself get better on her own, the way he did?

Alicia found it hard to understand Rick's viewpoint, especially when she knew that he cared about her in other ways. They recalled the first time in their marriage when she had been ill for weeks with the flu. He'd made sure he was out of the house most of the time, allowing her—from his point of view—to get better in peace. Only when she had asked him, in tears, why he wasn't looking after her, had she prevailed upon him to nurse her. Though he relented, he found her too demanding. Clearing up what *support* meant to each of them individually went a long way to reducing both expectation and disappointment in this marriage, but more work was needed.

In sessions with Alicia, we explored a cord she had with Rick. She came to realize that when she was ill herself or when she was nursing him, she was unconsciously siphoning off her worry and anxiety onto her husband. When she was a child, she had felt she could rest in her mother's care. As an adult she was unconsciously looking for this whenever excessive stress in her life—usually as a result of taking on too much—made her ill. Her mother's attention had allowed her to relax, unlike Rick's reaction, which was to get tense, feeling something was expected of him, even if he was the one being nursed.

As Rick recuperated from his accident, Alicia was worried and stressed by his incapacitated state. She transferred her stress back to him in an unconscious habit of off-loading responsibility for her own emotional state onto others. This dynamic made Rick become more aloof from her, to try to keep some space for himself.

After clearing the cord, Alicia reported feeling less needy. She felt more able to support herself emotionally, and was more trusting in Rick's being able to handle his own state. She was also taking care not to get too stressed. We followed that by clearing the cord she still had to her mother.

It was not until Rick had to have a hernia operation a few months later that they both observed marked changes in the way she was looking after him. Rick happily reported that Alicia asked what he needed first before bustling in, was more respectful of his rest time, and gave help, meals and attention only when he wanted them. Both of them were happier because Alicia realized she was giving what he needed and Rick recovered rapidly. And most happily, for Alicia, Rick responded to her increasing independence by becoming more aware of when she needed his consideration, and giving it without feeling it as a demand.

There is an intriguing development to this ongoing story. Rick's father died suddenly of a stroke, and he and Alicia traveled overseas for the funeral. Alicia told me on their return she now understood, having met Rick's family for only the second time since their wedding, why Rick was often so unemotional. Not one of the bereaved family cried or showed any signs of grief while she was there. However, when Rick and Alicia returned to their hotel room, Rick sat motionless and silent on his own, still absorbing the shock of his father's sudden death. Seeing this, Alicia sat silently next to him, holding his hand. To her surprise, Rick turned to her with tears pouring down his face. Neither of them said a word, she simply held him while he sobbed.

I asked Rick what he had been feeling at that moment and he said it was the first time as an adult that he had allowed himself to feel so deeply. After discussing this for a while, Rick realized that the stiff stoicism and coldness with which his family normally related had conditioned him to bear his suffering in silence and alone. Rick had felt intense pain in his heart at the time of his father's death, and while the ache was still there, it was gradually reducing in what he felt was a natural way. He was no longer resisting feeling whatever was coming up in him.

It was the beginning of a new chapter in Rick's life. One in which he found that allowing emotion to flow through him hurt far less in the long run, and took less energy, than suppressing how he was feeling.

There are times when being strong is important. Then it is necessary to suspend feeling our pain and emotion—temporarily—so they don't decrease our ability to cope. Our brain will do this for us, as the central controller of all the pain we feel. When Rick let Alicia's deep empathy reach him, when he relaxed instead of pushing his emotions away for fear of being weak, he allowed himself an emotional release. In the end he felt more whole. He could be more loving and more appreciative of Alicia. He now sees resilience as more important than resistance to pain and emotion.

The cord between Rick and Alicia used to mean a constant flow of intense expectation, worry, disappointment, irritation and neediness back and forth without resolution. Since the cord clearing, each of them has worked on differentiating themselves as emotionally mature adults, able to soothe themselves, but also to be there supportively for the other when needed.[24] Caring for each other no longer means their emotions merge; now, along with good communication, they empathically understand what the other is feeling.

DEALING WITH DEMENTIA

Marita looked after her aged mother for years until her dementia became too much for Marita to deal with alone. Though she didn't feel good about it, Marita finally admitted that the constant worry and the need to be there 24/7 in case her mother wandered off or fell was too much for her. She moved her mother to a nursing home, where she visited her every day, even though her mother no longer knew her. Her mother often complained to her that no one visited, as though she were a stranger. It hurt Marita deeply.

Lately Marita had been experiencing a marked absentmindedness, with gaps in her memory. She would forget what she was saying in the middle of a sentence, why she'd gone into a particular room or what she needed at the supermarket. She often lost her keys and had alarming thoughts that she hadn't turned off the iron or the gas, because she couldn't remember doing so.

These could have been symptoms of depression, but even though Marita was only in her 40s, she was convinced she was somehow catching her mother's dementia.

It made her feel even guiltier, because she no longer wanted to visit her mother. It was such hard work, and hurtful, since her mother didn't recognize her and often snapped angrily at her, as she did at the staff.

When Marita came for her first session, she commented that she wanted to save her mother from suffering and that she consciously let her mother draw on her strength. But lately, she had been feeling that it was draining her beyond what she could bear. Since she had no rational basis for this, she wondered whether it was all just her imagination. If she withdrew her energetic support, would her mother suffer?

As the session proceeded, Marita saw a cord in the form of a tangled tumbleweed of confusion that filled the space around their two heads whenever she was with her mother. It was there even when she was elsewhere and just thought of her mother. Instead of giving her mother energy and strength, Marita saw that she was merely the unconscious dumping ground for her mother's mental confusion. This then flowed back to her mother, along with Marita's guilt and grief, whenever she drew on her daughter's energy. So the cord was neither helping her nor fulfilling Marita's loving intention.

After I cleared the cord, Marita stayed away from the nursing home for three days. At that point she got a call from the nurse, who said that Marita's mother was surprisingly lucid that day. She was asking for Marita, saying she hadn't seen her for three days. Used to her mother's not knowing who she was or whether she had visited,

Marita had some trepidation in going to the nursing home. To her amazement, though, her mother was alert and seemingly in full possession of her senses. Marita took her out for a drive and it was the happiest and most relaxed she had seen her for some time.

The nurse warned her that her mother's dementia might return at any time, and that it was more or less normal to have patches of lucidity. Nevertheless, Marita had never seen such a big change, and believed it was because of the clearing, not simply a coincidence.

When her mother's dementia did return, Marita commented to me that her new level of perception had allowed her to detach from her mother's confusion. She no longer allowed herself to feel guilty and, though sad, she accepted her mother's deteriorating state. Her own confusion was far less, though she still felt its resonance when she visited twice a week and tuned in to her mother.

Chapter 29

Our attachments and Characters

In his early 20s, Jonathan is a hard worker, apprentice to a builder. He's a serious young man, in love with Suki, who recently broke up with him because, she told him impatiently, their relationship wasn't progressing.

Jonathan was devastated. He had no idea their relationship wasn't perfect just as it was. After all, didn't she understand he had to work hard for a few years to build up the kind of savings that would allow them to build their own house, have kids and a decent lifestyle?

Apparently, Suki wanted everything—the house, the money—RIGHT NOW. It was the Fairy Tale Princess Character, wanting the magical white wedding with seven bridesmaids, the extended European honeymoon in the Greek islands or, at the very least, Fiji. But, closely entwined with that was an Abandoned Waif Character that needed assurances that they would be together forever, that life would always be happy and that their love would last, no matter what.

Suki knew logically that such an idealistic idea was impossible, but she found herself in knots of anxiety that she might never get what she so desperately wanted. Most of the time she spent with Jonathan, she felt bitter disappointment. She was unable to enjoy being in the present moment, or to trust their future to unfold with confidence that they would handle whatever came along. When she ended it, she cited his lack of ambition and achievement as the reason.

Jonathan tried everything he could to talk to Suki, to reason with her, but she was unmovable. She went on a trip back to Japan to see family and to get over him, leaving him heartbroken.

When Jonathan came to see me he was sad about what he saw as his lost chance. He was convinced he'd never recover his lost love or the feeling of blissful belonging he'd had while with Suki. He moped about how wonderful things were in the past and wished he could have them over again to appreciate them better.

Jonathan's emotions were intense, and he had reason to feel sad and disappointed. However, the one who was talking in his head was the Tragic Romantic Character, who was lost in the past. He was unable to see anything of value in the present moment.

To change his mood, I asked him what he loved to do. Surfing, he said, though, significantly, it had been a few months since he had taken time for his favorite pastime. I gave him some homework. Go surfing as soon as you can. Be in the experience, in the present. Pay attention to the sounds of wind and surf and seagulls around you. Feel the water, the temperature and softness of it, and the sensations of the water surging and falling under your board. See the sun's reflection glinting on the surface. Smell the salty air. Watch the clouds in the sky and notice the colors. Enjoy the moment.

So Jonathan went to the coast for a weekend. Out in the ocean, wholly enjoying the experience of surfing, he was able to forget about Suki and his lost chance for the first time since she left.

By practicing being in the present, Jonathan was gradually able to appreciate his life now. He was able to put their relationship into perspective and was able to let it go.

Then Suki came back. She left a message, asking to see him. In our next session, Jonathan was anxious about what he should do. I asked him what he wanted and he answered that he dreamed of their getting back together. We talked about what he wanted to keep in the relationship and what he wanted to leave behind, and the possibility of creating the relationship he wanted in the present, on a whole new level.

Jonathan was surprised when he and Suki saw each other again. He was no longer anxious, and she was also different. She seemed more in the present, too, and wanted to enjoy what they had together without unrealistic expectations of the future. She still wanted the wedding, the house, the kids, but she could wait. And by focusing on the present she was able to see that Jonathan was really the one for her.

The reason Suki changed, of course, was because of Jonathan's energy, which was transmitted along their cord. Because he'd changed, too—and they were both open to it—it had enabled their whole relationship to change. Life became fun and exciting once more.

Jonathan and Suki's story shows how it is possible to evolve within the same relationship. It's neither a simple nor an automatic process. But being in the present with each other makes it so much easier to leave old patterns of behavior behind. And this was one case that didn't need a clearing.

Recently, Jonathan came to see me again about another matter. As we caught up with everything that had happened, I asked how things were going with Suki. He described how close they'd become, and how there had been a huge test when she'd had to return to Japan to be with her dying grandmother for a few weeks. They'd missed each other terribly and Jonathan was aware of Suki from a distance, drawing on him energetically for comfort in the lonely distress of waiting for her grandmother's death. He consciously allowed this, happy to provide what she needed, feeling they were both in the present as they did this.

I knew he'd really made a breakthrough, though, when he described how, when he was particularly low one day, he'd remembered a happy time with Suki. It was just a moment, he said, when they'd felt very close: a sunrise on a remote beach, with the sun tinting water and sky pink and gold, and the sand a soft gray. He told me how this memory of extraordinary beauty flooded him with peace and allowed him to deal effectively and in the moment with the situation he was finding difficult.

How was this different from when he was living in regret for the past? Jonathan was able to fully enter this memory of a shared special time because he had been completely in the present then. It was a golden moment, a few minutes that shone with a special completeness. There was no regret that he was not able to have Suki or any other part of that moment there now. The joy of that past moment in the present transcended time and enabled him to be more here, now.

Chapter 30

Forgotten pacts

In the deep reflective space of the Inner Eye, clients will often uncover a pact they've made in their childhood or the long forgotten past, with themselves, to be or act in a certain way from that point onward. It's a solemn resolve, frequently made at a time of trauma, injustice or following a bitter realization or disillusionment. Such pacts are generally made to protect the person in the future.

The promises are usually along the lines of "If that's the way it is," they will say sorrowfully, "then from this moment I will act as though . . ." or "I'll never let anyone get close enough to hurt me again" or "I will never let anyone see me weak again." These moments can be the basis for the formation of a particular Character that we believe will keep us safe. So we may end up with the manipulative Little Girl Character who plays a timid girly role around men, or a tough, Aloof Character that affects not to care. Such decisions can have a powerful, unseen, ongoing effect. Years later the unfortunate person discovers they have built a rigid armor that limits their creativity, encases their freedom and narrows their power of choice. Since as human beings we learn best by our mistakes and grow strong and wise through painful lessons, this rigid armor restricts our growth by preventing us from being vulnerable.

Binding pacts can be made with others, as well. In past-life regression sessions, it's not unusual for clients to uncover an ancient romantic vow intended to bind them for eternity or perhaps in servitude to a religion. We might feel the ongoing influence of these vows, even when the task of the present life is radically different. Only when we rediscover the long-ago pact we made and release it can we be free once more to begin the journey to be whole.

In this solemn moment, encountering what we have deliberately or inadvertently done to ourselves in the past, we can make a new pact with ourselves to let go. Although we cannot change the past, we can make a new decision that will affect our lives from this point on. If our new pact is created with as much solemnity and sincerity as the previous pact, it will be binding. And if we can remember and acknowledge the creativity that we've used to find a way through past difficulties, we can build on this experience to grow and flourish. We can choose a freer path to joy and love that honors our Self in the present.

Human beings are best when we are resilient, bending with the wind but not breaking, adapting to situations while remaining true to who we are. Being "open" does not necessarily mean being vulnerable—it means letting things flow through us without significance or resistance. We can be as irrepressible as those Mandarin dolls called *bu dao weng* with the weighted, rounded bottoms. Tip them over, watch them right themselves, again and again, smiling their secret smile. The knack is to roll with the punches. Life lessons that are torturous when we resist them are far less painful when we decide instead to use them for growth and expansion.

Unless we are able to pinpoint the hold the past has over us, it can impact us in all kinds of insidious ways. Emma felt she was fully over David, who had been unbearably possessive and jealous throughout their relationship. Over the next couple of years she found two men she really liked, but the relationships faded one after the other. The men seemingly lost interest soon after a sexual relationship began.

After her latest boyfriend, Lars, told her about a weird experience he had had with her while lovemaking, she brought him along to investigate the problem. Like Emma, Lars was an experienced meditator. He had never before encountered what he described to Emma and me in the session. He admitted he was a little freaked out by it.

It was as though something didn't want him to make love to Emma, he said. During their lovemaking he had felt a fierce energetic attack on his penis. It was a hateful energy, he said, like sharp, biting teeth. At first he had withdrawn, confused, wondering whether Emma was fully willing to make love. When she assured him she was more than willing, he had tried to continue, only to feel an even fiercer antagonistic force trying to keep him out.

In the myths of several cultures there exists the idea of *dentata*—or teeth in the vagina of a fearsome, dominating woman. In psychoanalytic terms, the concept vagina dentata is considered to indicate a fear of castration. Lars found this puzzling; he had never experienced even the thought before. He maintained he hadn't ever worried about castration, and wasn't now—well, not enough to stop him from making love to Emma.

In their joint session, Emma realized that the energy Lars was describing was exactly the way her jealous ex-boyfriend David behaved. She began to map what soon emerged as a toxic cord. It appeared that David had wanted to make sure that if he couldn't have her, no one would.

To her dismay, Emma discovered a beast resembling a dragon guarded her vagina. That it was made of energy instead of flesh and blood didn't reduce its ferocity at all. She felt its teeth snap angrily when she thought of making love to Lars.

David had deliberately put it there, she felt, in his sperm. But she grew puzzled as they had always used condoms.

She had seen the dragon with a milky white consistency like "energetic semen" that David had deposited as a marker to keep other men away. If Lars had not been so perceptive, Emma would probably never have discovered this cord. She then remembered that since they had split, even though she had asked him to stop calling, David had an uncanny and annoying habit of calling her the next day after she had had sex with another man. The cord between them had evidently let him know what was happening.

In the follow-up session two weeks after clearing this cord, Lars reported that the dragon was definitely gone. Though David had called and left a series of messages for Emma in the three days after the clearing—which she had not returned—he had not called since.

It's not uncommon for this proprietorial kind of attachment to show up in a sexual context. The insecurities that invariably set up the formation of a cord are most exposed and threatened in the intimacy of a sexual relationship.

Nor is it unusual for a person on the other end of a cord—who doesn't want to let go—to try to reestablish contact right after a cord clearing. It happens often, even when that person has no idea about the clearing and no other contact with their former partner. On some level they feel the disconnection—which in many cases they try quite desperately to reestablish.

When the cord is no longer being fed from the other end, however, it no longer works. The connection has been broken.

Chapter 31

Are deliberate cords okay?

Once we become aware of cords and what they are creating in our lives, it's best to avoid them, regardless of whether they are toxic or not. We can cultivate cord-free relationships. We just need to differentiate ourselves from others, which can be difficult in the beginning.

If we do deliberately form or maintain a cord, it is more than likely to be inadvertently misused, even when we feel we are only ever loving. It is not called the unconscious mind for nothing! Often we are simply not aware of what we might be transmitting. If there is some unstated anger or tacit resentment that might be flowing along a cord to or from someone we love, increasing our self-awareness helps us know this. We can practice self-awareness until it becomes second nature.

A better alternative to a cord is to expand our personal space to include someone else—as in the exercise at the end of Part 3 (see page 226). It is far easier to sense clearly what they are feeling if we do this. After such an expansion we tend to bring our space back closer around ourselves in a natural, elastic response to what is needed. It is a skill used particularly by therapists, counselors and nurses, but also by teachers, group leaders, public speakers and performers. When they expand their space over the entire group or audience, they can sense what the audience needs and give it to them. They can immediately sense confusion or disaffection as well as pleasure and adjust their performance or delivery accordingly. Please note that this practice is not one of putting a boundary around others, or even a "bubble" or some such visualization, but a radiating expansion of our Egoic energy from our core, which allows others to be them Selves just as we are.

ORIENTEERING IN THE SPACE OF CONSCIOUS AWARENESS

Camp counselor and teacher Max took groups of teenage boys orienteering and on camping survival trips. Over ten nights in the wilderness, kids were encouraged to find solutions to problems and work out directions using compasses, maps and natural landmarks. They had to survive on the water supplies placed at predetermined checkpoints, rations they carried and any local food they found. The trip was designed to teach self-reliance and survival skills, grounded in a basic course they had received prior to setting out. While safety precautions were in place, a certain amount of risk was expected. The boys were in groups of five, and elected their own leader. There was a different leader every day so that each boy had two turns at leadership a few days apart.

Emotionally, such trips always had a pressure cooker effect as survival Characters emerged and the teenagers' self-esteem was tested.

Max was there as an observer and for emergencies only. Energetically, he had his feelers out over the entire group, the whole ten days and nights. It let him know how they were going, individually and in their collective mood. He kept track of the kids as they confronted physical obstacles and dealt with intense personality differences, but kept out of their way.

On one trip, one youngster, Nick, made himself an outsider, setting up a situation of "me against them" with his suspicious and alienating attitude. On the third day, he was missing from camp at daybreak. His one-man tent was empty, his pack gone. During the early hours of the morning Max had felt him stirring—energetically— and without letting the boy know, followed him as he left the camp. When he saw that Nick had hidden himself not far away under a rocky overhang in his sleeping bag, Max decided to use this as an exercise in team responsibility.

He went back to the camp and at first light woke the other boys, telling them that Nick had gone and that they had to find him and bring him back for breakfast. While angry and complaining at Nick's attention-seeking behavior, they set off in pairs to look for him. It took them much of the morning, but eventually the pair that found Nick were the boys whom he hated the most.

While Nick had set himself up as Victim, he had created a united front of Allied Persecutors against him in the others. It was a cord operating between them on the dynamic of resentment that led the two who found him to his hiding place. The cord intensified the venom between them, making it difficult to separate.

Over a late breakfast, the boys took turns to air their grievances, with Max mediating and insisting on only two rules: that everyone stayed till they worked this out, and that only words and no physical violence were used. It took time for them to vent all their anger. Eventually they calmed down enough to broach some positive solutions. The group decided that Nick would be leader the next day, to encourage his taking more responsibility and to redress his feelings of being an outsider.

At first, Nick behaved like a team of one. He failed to communicate what he wanted, then hotly criticized the rest of the boys. Max intervened just once, sharing with him privately how to expand his feelers over the whole group to see how he could better lead them. Surprisingly, this had a huge impact on Nick. By the end of the day he was beginning to show new qualities of consideration and leadership. His next turn at leadership showed a completely different boy.

Nick later considered this trip to be a turning point in his whole life. Though he didn't always succeed in his new attitude, he now knew he had a choice. Consciously putting his feelers out over the group he was leading had made him forget his own self-absorption for a period of time. In taking responsibility for the group, his personal concerns took perspective. He asked Max if he could go on other trips. Over time, through modeling himself on Max's low key and inclusive leadership style, his old habits of antagonism and dumping venom into cords began to break down.

SOMETHING'S NOT RIGHT . . .

Stephanie was a normal teenager who at 15 was pushing the boundaries of parental approval. Her mother, Talia, whose story we have followed at crucial times during her life in this book, was a meditator who often deliberately had to ignore intuitive knowledge of what her daughter was up to. If Stephanie became aware of her mother's insights, it would push the young girl into even more outrageous rebellion. So Talia often bit her lip and let the knowledge go. After all, Stephanie needed to learn her own boundaries and act responsibly. Most of the time it seemed that this was okay, and Stephanie's activities were not outrageously risky. There were two occasions, however, when Talia was deeply thankful that she could sense what was happening to her young rebellious teenager.

Stephanie was supposedly on a sleepover nearby with three girlfriends. At about 9:00 p.m., with no warning, Talia received a strong telepathic distress signal from Stephanie and immediately got into her car and, following inner promptings, drove to the local park. On the swings under park lights she saw Stephanie's three girlfriends and three young men she vaguely recognized from the neighborhood. As she pulled up in her car, she heard wild giggling and loud voices, but Stephanie was nowhere to be seen. She drove once more around the park, and it was on the second time around that she saw Stephanie emerging at a run, alone, from a alley near where she had stopped.

Using all her awareness, Talia sensed Stephanie from her car. There was no more distress around her, just some residual fear and a greater feeling of relief. Talia watched as Stephanie stopped briefly to talk to her girlfriends before the girls all left and walked back to the sleepover house nearby. The boys yelled insults after them and remained in the park. Before Talia drove off, another young man loped across the road and joined the group.

When Stephanie returned home the next day, neither of them mentioned the incident. It wasn't until a few years later that Stephanie told Talia her version of the events. An older boy that Stephanie liked, who'd had a few drinks, had enticed Stephanie to look at his car. There he had kissed her. In the romance of the moment, Stephanie had not worried until he'd begun pressing her for more. He began to use force, pushing her into the backseat, and she grew frightened. She kneed him in the groin and pushed him away. Running from the car, she had emerged from the alley where Talia had seen her.

While Talia wondered whether she would have found Stephanie in time, Stephanie commented that when he began forcing his attention on her, she knew all she had to do was get away. Almost immediately she had then felt safe. "It was like I was being looked after, Mom," she said. Then Talia related her side of it.

Comparing the two stories, Talia realized she had received foreknowledge of Stephanie's distress—since she had apparently arrived at the park at the exact moment Stephanie realized she was in trouble. It was a clear awareness for both of them as they understood the power of their connection. Stephanie looked at her mother for an instant and gave her a hug.

The second incident occurred a few months later. This time it was far more dangerous and Talia and her husband had intervened to prevent an almost certain violent gang rape. Again, it was Talia's foreknowledge that Stephanie was in danger that had prompted them to go looking for their daughter. Following this, Stephanie's behavior was much less wild. She had been well and truly frightened by what might have happened. It helped, too, that Talia gently communicated to her just what she had gone through in looking for her.

When Stephanie was not in danger, Talia had no need to know what was happening with her daughter. As the young girl grew older, Talia was able to withdraw even further to give her daughter the space she needed as an increasingly independent adult, as she had done with all her children.

Chapter 32

Living in the present

Have you ever found yourself staring out the window of a bus and had no awareness of what was going on around you for your entire journey? Perhaps you have experienced driving or walking somewhere and your thoughts were preoccupied, somewhere or some*when* else, the entire time. Suddenly you are at your destination with no idea of how you actually got there. Where were you? Your thoughts and perhaps emotions have taken you out of present time.

A friend, dating again after the breakup of a long-term relationship, described how horrified she was when she absentmindedly kissed her date on the cheek at the end of the night in exactly the way she'd been used to kissing her ex-husband. What disturbed her most was that she was so automatic in her response to this man she barely knew. She realized she had not been present the entire night. If we are used to living in unresolved emotions and thoughts from the past, we have little chance of connecting in real time and in a genuine way, with anyone. Any thought or emotion may be linked to a memory. At such a time, you are in the past, experiencing to a degree whatever you felt back then.

Be careful, for we can get lost in this, the past blurring with the present. While it is an excellent conscious process to discharge past wounds in therapy, it is not good to lead our lives like this. It is definitely no way to maintain a healthy relationship. The more present we are, the more in control of our lives we will be and the more our relationships will be as we intend them to be. In a therapy session, we can concentrate on resolving the past. In our lives, we need to be in the present. It's a state of awareness where we observe with all our attention in the here-and-now, without a thought or an emotion, but seeing, feeling, sensing, responding. Some practice in being in the present helps.

Subtle body awareness exercise 3: Experiencing a present time connection

These exercises involve grounding yourself in present time and expanding on the awareness you gained in the first two exercise sections. You can practice the first one below anywhere, anytime, alone or in company.

1. As you read this, perhaps you are sitting or lying down comfortably. Wherever you are, don't change your position, simply become aware of your body on the surface beneath you. Be aware of the pressure of your body on that surface, the hardness of your bones within your body. Become aware of the book in your hand, the color and texture of the paper, or if you are reading it on electronic or digital media, touch the screen and the surfaces surrounding it. Then shift your awareness to the surface on which you are sitting or lying. With a hand or foot, feel the temperature and texture of the material. Is it soft? Smooth? Warm? Firm? Is it a hard chair or floor? The more you can feel of the texture and temperature of these physical surfaces and objects, the more you will pull your mind and awareness into the present. If you find yourself having a thought, it will pull you away from this present time experience. If that thought leads you to an emotion, gently bring yourself back to experiencing some specific aspect of the physical universe—the texture of the material you are touching, its temperature, consistency, color, shape, contours, weight. How do you feel after the exercise? Do you notice you are more alert?

2. For this exercise you will need to sit comfortably alone, where you will not be disturbed for up to an hour. Begin by closing your eyes and

grounding your awareness in your body where it touches the surface on which you are sitting. Take time to feel the connection between your body and the physical universe. Breathe deeply and easily, adjust your body where it is not relaxed, bring yourself to a calm state.

Going within, find the part of you that feels like your core, where the real you lives. It varies for all of us, so take your time. You may feel it in your heart, your solar-plexus just under your ribcage, your belly (the area below your navel) or your Third Eye. Wherever it is, it will have an unmistakeable feeling of "this is the real me." You may feel it as an area of warmth, a flame, a spark or just an area of denseness or solidity. Everyone will feel it in a unique way, there is no wrong or right here.

Gently hold this area in nonphysical hands. Feel its contours and shape, its weight and texture, what it's made of. Cup it in your nonphysical hands and perhaps it might begin to expand. Allow it to expand to fill your torso, then your whole body from top to toe and finally the etheric body around your physical body. Without any attempt to imagine it or make it do so, allow it to continue expanding until it fills the egg—your astral body—around your physical body. This is your personal space. There's no rush and there should be no effort with this. If you lose the sense of it, go back to the place in your body where you felt the real you, cup it again in nonphysical hands and gently allow it to expand once more. Just experience the natural expansive principle of this, your real Self.

Going further, and when you feel comfortable to do so, allow the sense of your own presence to expand into the whole room. Sense the walls, the furniture in the room, the ceiling and floor. Fill the space with your presence. How does it feel? If it feels uncomfortable to be so expanded, gently bring your space back to where it feels comfortable around you. You may need to practice this often to feel truly comfortable. Open your eyes. Does this make a difference? Practice expanding your space with your eyes open.

3. The last exercise in this section is about sharing our space intentionally, and you will need a partner. Stand facing your partner at arm's length, in turns as A and B. First, take some time to ground yourself as in the previous exercises, with eyes closed. Feel your core and gently expand until your space is around your physical body. When you feel comfortable, open your eyes and hold your partner in soft-focus eye contact. The first partner then extends their space over and around the other person. Each of you note how it feels. Then the second partner has a turn. Open your eyes and exchange impressions.

Then, by intention, and without moving physically, speaking or signaling in any way, practice excluding the other from your space by creating space between you. Notice how you do this. After a few minutes of this, exchange impressions.

Then do it at the same time. Each of you create space between you while maintaining eye contact. How does it feel? Now slowly move apart, increasing physical as well as astral distance between you, and note how it feels. When you are as far away as the room you are in will allow, switch to putting your space around the other. Stay where you are for a moment, see if you can feel each other. Maintaining eye contact, begin to draw the other closer, by intention only. When you are an arm's length from each other, exchange impressions. Then slowly move apart again, still with your space around the other, maintaining eye contact. See how far away you can go before you lose the sense of the other in your space, or you in the other's space. From this distance, now practice pulling the other closer once more.

When we can do this at will and by intention we are less likely to do it unconsciously, and we are less likely to require cords to feel connected.

Part four

Meeting the World with Confidence

LIKE a dance that adapts to all the music in the world, we reach toward each other and move apart only to move closer, we lift and turn, flash with passion or hold with strength and tenderness. Whether in individual steps or in unison, our movements are in harmony with the melody of our lives.

Chapter 33

Creating me, creating you, creating us

A marriage or partnership is a good one if both of you are committed to the third universe of your relationship and to your own personal universe. Taking responsibility for your own happiness, you can support each other openheartedly without any obligation other than your own choice. You are able to express yourselves as individuals without being limited by the other. It's an excellent partnership if each of you is still interested in what your partner thinks and does, and if sex is even better between you than in your early years—in fact it keeps getting better. It should, as things do when we stay in constant practice with the intention of improving!

A great partnership is one in which each of you brings your whole self into the third universe, and can go back just as happily to your own personal universe. Far from the compulsive giving that ends with our being depleted and exhausted, this is about conscious giving from fullness, from an inexhaustible supply that doesn't come from the astral, etheric or physical bodies, but from the Ego, spirit incarnate.

We create ourselves by expressing ourselves creatively. Every time we take a course, follow a passion or an interest, meditate, read for enjoyment or information, attend a performance, travel, cook, write, play, paint, dance, sing or do something with someone else, we are creating ourselves. Actually, we have the choice of creating ourselves as a developing, evolving person or continuing habitual, unhelpful patterns, which only add to the manipulation and dysfunction of Characters and Character Games. At a certain point in our personal growth, it becomes impossible to go back to this old, dysfunctional way of being.

But how do we know that what we are trying to develop or grow in ourselves is the real us and not just wishful thinking, a fantasy?

Significant clues to who we really are may be in what we admire in others. This is not envy or jealousy. It's a feeling that creates pleasure, expansion and joy when we see something we admire, whether it's a quality such as courage, or an innate charm or way of being.

Envy, on the other hand, creates a feeling of contraction inside us. It's a feeling of being or having less, accompanied by the conviction that we will probably never have what others have that is so desirable. If we find ourselves envious, admiration can actually help us out of this dwindling spiral of self-hatred. We need to direct our attention away from what we believe we don't have, toward something about ourselves that we admire. Sometimes, this can be difficult to find.

The thing is, though, it really doesn't matter how small or trivial that special something we are or do is. Find something in yourself that pleases you. Maybe it's a quality you have that other people seem not to value, so you've stopped valuing it, too. Start acknowledging that wonderful quality you have. Maybe this quality is an attribute or a physical thing. Do you have a lovely smile? Great hair? Strong muscles? One client told me the only thing she admired in herself was her slim, elegant ankles. So, that's where she started. With practice she was then able to find other things she valued about herself, including her warm heart. The expansive energy of admiration increased her ability to find myriad wonderful things about herself and others. She felt even better about herself, realizing that she was actively changing her old negative thinking in the process.

To turn things around, you can create the right mind-set by intention, backed up by repeated affirmations such as "I let go of my fear and open to love" or "I release my past and totally love and accept myself." These affirmations might only remain effective for a short time—but that's when your intention and your Will come together more uniformly, and you'll have created a more supportive climate of self-esteem.

Admiration creates what it admires. This means that if we value courage, openheartedness, generosity of spirit, confidence, good humor and enthusiasm in someone else, it reinforces and strengthens those qualities in ourselves. In fact, if we didn't have the qualities we admire in others within us already, they would not resonate with us so powerfully. We might not even notice them. Admiration leads to aspiration, as we aim to be more of what we admire in others.

It's often the case that what we admire in a prospective partner is how we aspire to be. In fact, it's heartening to know that their qualities often reflect how we really are—beneath our old conditioning that has made us insecure or unconfident. We might yearn for someone who is self-assured but not arrogant, confident and realistic about their own abilities, happy to be on their own or in company, enthusiastic about life and able to enjoy themselves.

At this stage, however, these qualities in ourselves may be undeveloped. Our aspirations for them let us know this. If our aspiration is accompanied by a serious intention that that is what we want, it's a positive development in which we have a good chance of achieving our aims.

If we take notice of what we admire in others and start consciously to create those qualities in ourselves, we will find we don't need others to complete us. In fact, it is the act of loving someone that completes us, rather than finding someone else to fill that gap we feel within ourselves. We do need to be well-matched—which means that if we have a high level of self-determination and confidence and our partner matches us in those, the unconscious mind games and control games that create cord relationships will not be necessary. The partnership has a chance to be equal. If it is, it has a chance to last.

LEARNING TO TRUST OURSELVES

When Hana started working on herself in psychotherapy, she realized that the main feature of all her relationships was control. She was attracted to men who let her do whatever she wanted. Most of the men were followers, not leaders. But they never lasted, so Hana wasn't happy. She got bored. One way or another she found herself in the push-pull of subtle control games. Then she'd despise her partners for being weak.

She began by working on her deeply buried fear that she wasn't good enough. Gradually she built confidence by practicing acknowledging her strengths. She addressed her terror of losing control, which was really about being disliked and left alone. In the past she had compensated for this by asserting she didn't need anyone. It meant she couldn't accept compliments. Conditioned by criticism and ridicule in her childhood, her low self-image meant that when people complimented her, she believed they were mocking her, so she would scoff or make a sarcastic remark. If they meant it, Hana assumed it signified that their expectations of her would be higher still. There was therefore a greater potential to disappoint. To control this uncomfortable feeling of overwhelming expectations on her, she would minimize the praise or attribute it to someone else. Hana's first challenge was simply to accept compliments graciously.

Systematically turning her attention to past, unresolved cords, Hana had them cleared one by one. When this phase was completed, I asked her to draw three columns on a blank sheet of paper. The first column was to be headed My Ideal Partner. Under that, using the awareness she had gained of herself, she made a list of the qualities she wanted in a partner. It was such a long list that Hana had some uncertainty about whether she was being too demanding, too idealistic. I reminded her that this was her ideal mate, no one else's. She began her list with *kind*, and continued with *no mind games, in touch with his feelings, a good communicator, a good sense of humor, intelligent, a good lover, financially independent, faithful* and so on.

When Hana looked at her ideal partner on paper, she realized that if he were to walk in at that moment, she would panic. She knew she would immediately doubt that he would be interested in her. She was afraid he would see in her all the failings she saw in herself.

In the second column, I asked her to rate herself, on a scale of one to ten, on each quality she wanted in her ideal partner. In some she rated herself highly. For every item in which she scored seven out of ten or less, I asked her to put an asterisk. These amounted to a personal self-improvement list on which she could work over a period of time. I asked her how long she thought she might need to improve on these qualities. She decided on a year. During this time she decided she would not allow herself to get involved in any romantic relationships. She was embarking on the process of creating herself as the person she wanted to be, as she truly was underneath. This was important work, so she didn't want any distractions.

Overall, Hana realized that she didn't really want to control in any compulsive way, or be controlled, but to approach each situation in her life with confidence in her own ability to handle whatever occurred. At the end of her celibate period, as if by magic, her ideal partner appeared on the scene. Actually, he had been around for some time in the background, but she had never thought of him as a candidate.

And here was when the third, until now empty, column in her list came into play. When he first asked her out, in a kind of wonder that she had never thought of him in this way, she mentally checked off all the qualities she had listed. She was delighted in the self-assured, emotionally mature man she had attracted simply by becoming more herself. To her great joy she discovered she was also, surprisingly, wildly attracted to him. He didn't play the covert control games she had experienced in all her previous romantic attachments. And most of the time, neither did she.

There was an adjustment phase. Sometimes she would feel the pull of her old habitual games and have to stop herself. It helped that with a laugh she was able to "name and shame" the Characters doing this—Miss Control Freak or the Hypercritic. By now Hana knew our Characters take over only when we abdicate our choices and our personal power, when we lose confidence in our own ability to handle things in the here and now. Whenever she found a Character saying something, in its usual, automatic reaction, she would tell herself to "rewind, erase, start again," reaching deeper into her inner reserves to get back in touch with how she really wanted to communicate and behave. Hana's confidence was growing in a genuine, empowered way and so, too, was her pride in being able to relate without the games that accompany cords.

One of Hana's most challenging hurdles was to learn to trust that her new partner would not be callous with her heart. It came as quite a revelation to her that she now knew he was someone she could trust. She wasn't projecting unrealistic fantasies onto him, and just hoping and wishing he'd be kind. It was something she could be sure of, because in dealing with her own illusions she'd developed a strong sense of truth and deception. And while he was also human, and occasionally wasn't kind, she knew his heart was good. In handling her own insecurities, Hana developed strength. If she found herself dwelling on what she lacked, she quickly changed her thinking. She no longer held on to the past for fear of not having it in the future. She'd begun to trust herself.

TIPS AND TRAPS

Many of my clients have done "The Ideal Partner List." Generally, the things they write down first are the most important to them. Strangely enough, these are often also the things that are ignored when it comes to a prospective partner. That is the first tip: Do not think that because most of the boxes are checked that you have found your Ideal Partner. You won't. You'll have more of what you've already had—because the very thing that blinds us to what is the real truth condemns us to repeat the same mistakes.

At the top of Rebecca's list was "Unattached." She'd found herself as Other Woman or Mistress in too many relationships. Now she felt ready to be Number One in her mate's eyes. The man she found seemed to match every single item on her list—until she found out one morning, having stayed the night at his house—that the man's ex-wife was there for breakfast. In fact, there had actually been no divorce yet, just a separation. The house belonged to his wife and she still lived there half the week when not away for work. Clearly the man's ties to his wife were still strong. Four years later, when I again met Rebecca, she told me she had only recently finally ended her relationship with this man. The odd arrangement between the man and his wife—still not divorced, still sharing a house—was unchanged. Even though when Rebecca made the list she fully intended to go only for an unattached man, she had not honored her most important wish—to be Number One, for herself and a partner. I was intrigued and asked her about it.

"Well, it was the only thing that wasn't perfect about him," she told me.

However, when she looked at her relationship in more detail, she realized there were many other things that weren't right, and that if she had honored herself more she would have noticed and not accepted this man as a partner in the first place. Interestingly, until then she had not even understood that she had managed to repeat the same old pattern. Having seen this, she was then more determined to never again accept "second best."

It helps to look at the Ideal Partner list in this way: if you are looking for a place to live and want a light, airy house on a hill with a view, you would not even look at a small, dark, damp studio apartment in a basement. For some of us, our fantasies about what will happen after we get married are as far away from the reality as this.

We compromise so many essentials that we end up with the dark basement apartment, hoping it will change.

One fascinating phenomenon that accompanies working on specific qualities in ourselves in any systematic way is that, just when we are working on, for example, increasing our compassion, we will attract people to us who desperately need that compassion—or whatever our current focus is. The trap is to avoid forming a relationship at that point. We're not cooked yet!

It goes without saying that honesty is essential in close relationships, but most of all with ourselves. If we have made an "Ideal Partner List" and have begun working on those asterisked qualities we want to change or improve in ourselves, we need to be sure we've actually achieved the change and not just hope we've done enough work on ourselves. So, it helps to ask ourselves when the period of time we've given ourselves for this work is coming to a close, "Am I cooked enough?" Look at who you are attracting at this point. With all the perception you have honed through self-examination, are they truly your ideal mate, checking off ALL the boxes? Remember, we attract those who are at our same level of evolution, so we can help each other grow. The acid test is whether we would feel worthy of our ideal mate if they were to walk in right then. If we feel we don't deserve the bad things that have happened, but are still somehow attracting them, then we need to look more closely at what we might be unconsciously putting out there, and tackle those, courageously and without blame. When we have improved all those qualities on our side of the list that we felt needed changing, we will know without the slightest doubt that we deserve our ideal mate.

Communication is an essential building block of all successful relationships. With it we can express what we feel and think; what we wish and hope for. We can inform others about what we are about to do. We can also withhold verbal communication while non-verbally conveying our thoughts and emotions perfectly clearly through our body language, facial expressions, frowns, averted looks, shining eyes, smiles, attentiveness or indifference.

When there is an energetic cord between us and another person, we can usually feel to some degree whether they are telling the truth or lying. Of course, we can do this if we are skilled at reading people and tuning in, but a cord is often the first mechanism by which we feel that first lack of congruence between what they say and what we feel from them, even if what they say is unexpected or painful. If it is a toxic cord, the knowledge of being lied to adds to betrayal. It creates uncertainty, fear and resentment, contributing to what is already noxious in the cord. However, if we are still living unawares in a fantasy universe and projecting that onto a partner, we tend to use a great deal of energy denying and suppressing what we know deep down of their deception. It can surface as vague anxiety and tension. It definitely requires our attention.

If we are in a fantasy universe, willfully deluding ourselves about the true nature of our partnership, then the plausible lies that come to us verbally or through the cord only feed our illusions. In turn, these lies create greater tension as we continue to avoid the truth even when we are in denial.

Learning how to communicate honestly depends on how well we know ourselves. Of course, there are degrees of openness. With strangers or casual acquaintances it might not be appropriate or wise to share the intimate details of our lives. There's a deeper level of openness that we are comfortable sharing with our family. Hopefully the deepest level is the one we share with our life partner. The more we know about ourselves, the more we can read trustworthiness in others and the more we can discern what is appropriate to communicate to family, friends and lovers. We can know who to trust, and for what.

When we are honest with ourselves, the truth that others speak does not hurt nearly as much as when they lie. Often we can know the truth before it is spoken, and have already begun to assimilate it, even when it is unpleasant. But a lie rankles, disturbing the peace and flow of a relationship. The same is true of any secret that we keep from our partner. If they or we are living through a Character, the way we communicate will be tinged with the falsity that surrounds all Characters—overdramatized and delusional to various degrees. Though our Characters believe their own delusions, we should not.

If honest communication depends on our knowing ourselves, how do we discover what we are telling ourselves and whether it is truth or illusion?

The answers lie in the deep stillness of meditation.

Chapter 34

What the real you has to say

Experienced meditators are more tuned than nonmeditators to receive information or impressions from their Higher Self. Often, this happens in everyday activities. There's a sudden thought we have forgotten something. We take something unusual with us on impulse when we leave the house or work, only to find later we need that very thing. This also happens in a more profound way in meditation.

The state of deep meditation is one of expanded space and presence of the Egoic body. In this state, the Column of Spirit that extends above from the crown chakra, through the Egoic body and into spiritual realms, becomes a conduit for information that is enlightened and inspired or simply marvelously instructional. This is one of the highest levels of cord—to our Higher Self, or what some call the Oversoul. Certain knowledge is made available to us about our lives or our direction, and we may take action accordingly. This higher knowingness needs no explanations or support of a lower, rational mind because it is so clearly right for us on all levels.

Sometimes the information coming from our Higher Self is about a radical change we need to make—such as leaving a relationship that has passed its use-by date—and closing a chapter in our lives so we can move on to the next. We need to pay attention to this. If we do not follow this inner knowingness about what is right for ourselves, the consequences can be unnecessarily painful.

If we are not aware on the higher level of the Egoic body, or if we ignore, suppress or deny it, this important information has to come closer to us, to where we might be more aware. It next shows up in our astral body—through our thoughts and emotions. It won't be as clear as in the higher perceptive state, but if we are paying attention to it, the information can give us valuable guidance in avoiding problems in every area of our lives, from our health, to relationships, to work. We'll feel this guidance perhaps as unease, or have unaccustomed thoughts, sudden intense emotions and flashes of realization connected to past patterns. We might have weird dreams that linger in our memory long after waking. Sometimes this manifests as stressful outbursts of unexplained emotion that indicate we are not giving ourselves enough rest—or some other element vital to our overall well-being. If it's about a relationship we need to move on from, this can manifest in strong criticism or anger toward our partner, violent arguments and periods of disharmony that nothing seems to fix. Sometimes simple honest communication can make a huge difference. Sometimes we can't find a way to communicate.

If we are not aware enough of our emotions or our thoughts, or if we ignore them or suppress them for whatever reason, the information has to come closer still, to our etheric body, the life force body. We experience the message here as fever, tingles, shivers and tremors, rapid temperature changes or giddiness. It can manifest as tinnitus or a high-pitched tone that is audible within our heads. Sometimes, on the edge of sleep or waking, we might feel we are enormous or very tiny relative to our physical body. It's all designed to alert us to something that needs our attention. By now, however, the information is difficult to decode. We now need to examine areas of our life we might be neglecting or misusing. Are we looking after ourselves as we should? Is our relationship nourishing us? Are we allowing ourselves to be mistreated, or are we mistreating ourselves?

If we are unaware of the effects of this communication on our etheric body, or if we ignore or suppress it, the information comes closer in, to rest in the form of energy blocks in our physical body. At first it might show up in acute injuries, infections or illnesses. It's telling you to wake up. Something is not as it should be.

For example, if there's a pattern of minor injuries to one side of your body—repeatedly stubbing your left toe, knocking your left elbow or shoulder—take note. Ruled by our right brain, the left side is traditionally the side of emotion and intuition, the home, the female part of us (whether we are male or female), or it can relate to interactions with one or more females in our life. Injuries to our left side might indicate a problem with an emotion or inner knowing or a female around us that we need to deal with. If injuries are repeated on the right side of the body, traditionally it relates to our work or interactions out in the world, or with men, or the male side of us. It can be about problems to do with or solved by rational thought. See if any of these are true for you or relevant to your situation.

Further physical-level information might come in the form of sudden serious health crises such as a heart attack or ministroke.

Fortunately, most people are alarmed enough by these manifestations to change their lifestyle to something kinder and healthier. If these warnings are ignored, they might then develop into chronic illnesses and more serious diseases. Terminal illnesses are the end result. It's not uncommon for people at this stage—finally and too late—to realize what they needed to act on long ago.

Naturally, not all accidents or severe illnesses are the result of this process. Sometimes it is just a matter of bad luck or being in the wrong place at the wrong time. Still, it pays to have a look, as repeated patterns give you a vital clue about what's happening to you at a whole other level than you were aware of. Is there something you need to act on now, to change your life before it is too late? It may be that your awareness is more acute than you think. Somewhere deep inside, you already know the answers.

It is natural to react with fear at the thought of something being wrong. Fear is designed to make us more alert. If we act on it, we can reduce the fear with an appropriate response—do what we know we should, get a diagnosis or treatment if needed—and reduce overall tension.

When it comes to looking for an energetic cord, these differing levels of awareness are significant. If you are a practiced meditator, it is far easier to make distinctions between your own energy and that of a cord.

If you find meditation difficult or even think it impossible for you, there is a middle step that might serve you well. Before you fall asleep, give yourself a command to remember your dreams. Put a pad and pen beside your bed to record your dreams as soon as you wake (and before you visit the bathroom, lest the memory fade). You can also do this with any images that come to you in the state between waking and sleeping. The images and symbols are directly from your intuitive right brain. Many creative people use this technique effectively, and often find the solution to a problem appearing the next morning.[25]

If you think about your relationship before you sleep, ask your right brain for information about any unhealthy attachment that might exist. Often the cord is represented in a way that makes it brilliantly obvious the next morning.

The most important thing when listening to your Self through meditation is not simply to guess what's going on. Just relax as you examine it. It's okay not to know what it means. Rest in the silence of the moment. Be open, receptive and the answer to what you're being shown will appear.

Chapter 35

The gifts of long-term meditation

Many think of meditation as simply a relaxation activity. This is misleading. Meditation is the practice of expanding consciousness and awakening our true spiritual nature. The operative words here are *consciousness* and *awakening*.

In beginners, it's about getting used to sitting in an unfamiliar posture, with breathing and focusing exercises to help concentration. We need to get used to sitting with a straight back to allow the regular flow of cerebrospinal fluid to and from the brain and the spinal cord, to maximize alertness.[26] If we tilt our hips forward and tail bone back, relaxing our shoulder and back muscles while sitting as tall as we can, we learn to let the spine hold us up instead of straining our muscles. Dipping our chin slightly also helps. Over time our body becomes accustomed to sitting in this economical way and tensions are lessened. Our mind becomes progressively quieter, clearer and less chaotic. There's less left-brain chatter. For beginners, this takes some getting used to.

It is definitely worth the persistence.

For experienced meditators, there's an increase in awareness of energy flow both within and around the physical body. The reactive mind, seated in the *amygdala* or mammalian limbic system of the brain, recedes. Emotions seem remote, while insight grows.

Still, there are seemingly endless distractions that take us out of the awareness of the present. If you find you are beset by what meditators call the "monkey mind" with its bewildering, mercurial flitting from one thought to another, the patient practice of observing thoughts and where they come from eventually slows them down. Unexpectedly, we realize that our thoughts rarely originate in our own mind, but drift in via many thought streams to which we may be already tuned in, or not. Those thoughts that match our emotional tone resonate in our own heads.

It's why, if we want to change the way we habitually think and feel, often the only way is to move out of a familiar location where ideas and points of view are rigid and restrictive. It's a meme, and we can be shaped by it via our susceptibility to the prevailing thought field.

Through the meditational practice of watching our thoughts, the habit of thinking every thought that might randomly float by is increasingly replaced by a state of expanded lucidity. Thoughts become like folders in our filing system. We can recognize them from the outside, and we no longer need to open them in an automatic fashion to see the contents and then get lost in them. It becomes easier to distinguish samskaric imprints and energy blocks that result from our past wounds. The state of relaxed, alert attention increases as we are enabled to be more in the richness of the present. The specific aspects of our subtle bodies become more apparent. We can tell the difference between our astral body with its flaring pyrotechnics and emotional turmoil, our etheric body, with its tingling vibrations and grasping for life, and the Egoic body of vast presence, deep peace and spiritual connections.

It is an entirely different state to ordinary waking consciousness—which in most of us is likely to be immersed in the overcerebration of the left brain and, often, the sensate confusion of the astral body. It's a state in which we can access the calm insight and creativity of the right brain.

In the expanded presence of the Egoic body through meditation, we can access a state of higher mental function. Lightning fast, connecting creative ideas of vastly different sources, limpid and infinitely calm, it may well be one of the first levels of what the great Indian sage Sri Aurobindo called the supramental consciousness, the next stage of man's evolution.[27]

There are some interesting results about meditation that come from neuroscientific testing using electroencephalographic imaging (EEG) of long-term meditators. It appears that during meditation all the brain waves are enhanced and increased, from slow relaxed alpha waves, to alert thinking beta waves, through creative, lateral thinking theta waves to the fast processing and often precognitive gamma waves. Since more of the higher functions of the brain are being activated than in nonmeditators, the possibility of awakening consciousness through meditation seems proved. At the same time, the emotional surges of the limbic system are markedly less in impact.[28]

It is important to note the fact that the brain is *plastic*—meaning it can learn and grow and incorporate change—shows that changes effected to the brain through consistent meditation practice are permanent.

In the Third Eye Inner Space techniques that I often use with clients, a simple alteration in breathing stimulates the larynx, which in turn stimulates the pineal gland, the physical organ relating to the Third Eye and to subtle vision. The pineal gland lies directly behind the spot between our eyebrows, in between the two hemispheres of the brain. Focused attention there creates a harmonious balance between the right and left hemispheres of the brain, increasing the functional activity of each. Thus this technique reinforces subtle perception and profound understanding. What in purely right-brain function is a blissful sense of oneness, appreciation of beauty and eternal existence, is married to the left brain's attention to detail and ability to see linear progression. We truly become more whole.

Chapter 36

Making sense of it all

I f we use ordinary reflection mode to look for cords, we might not
see much. What we do see, we might not understand. It makes
it easy to shrug off as complex. If we analyze an experience or a
drawing of what we have seen in our mind's eye from a psychological viewpoint we can surmise or deduce various aspects of what is
being expressed unconsciously. And experiencing it from a deeper
perspective like meditation, we'll see even more. Sometimes it's not
until later that we integrate what we've seen in our inner vision with
what we now understand. It can be like a dream full of symbols and
metaphors. Or it can be the mind's bizarre literal translations, such
as the sea of long grass in Talia's dream in Chapter 3, which is how
her mind interpreted the sea grass matting she saw in her dream.

In the Inner Space process, as in the profound stillness of meditation, deeper understanding can come with dazzling realizations
of what these symbols, metaphors and flashes of memory mean in
terms of our lives now and our direction for the future.

MAPPING THE TRUE DYNAMICS

Taking the time to map a cord—finding out its terrain, its "weather," shape and history—gives us an appreciable amount of information. Not only is there the opportunity to observe the energetic link and how it operates, it also tells us more about our relationship, its history and our status within it. We learn the flavor of the energy of a toxic cord and can recognize such and avoid becoming trapped by cords in the future.

When we put conscious attention on something—especially something energetic—it grows, in our awareness and in its presence in our life. If we are looking at something in ourselves and it is true—from our Higher Self—it remains as a permanent development within our energy. If it is false—that is, from a reactive, conditioned, samskaric source—it will first expand, becoming intense for a short period, then it will dissipate. Reactive emotions such as apathy, unresolved grief, shame, chronic pain, guilt, resentment, suppressed anger, neediness and heavily guarded fear all feel heavy. Higher feelings are lighter and mark the true Self: interest, acceptance, empathy, enthusiasm, serenity and unconditional love. As we observe it, a heavy emotion will discharge to the same degree that we are fully conscious of it and do not resist it. We are letting it go.

Because of this, cord observations are uncomfortable for a period of time, their effect is intensified by our scrutiny. However, it's also the way to defuse them. Consciousness discharges chaos—and the more consciousness we can bring to bear on a toxic cord or the samskara at its base—without resistance or reactions—the quicker its power dissolves.

Doing a drawing of the cord can be helpful in defining what

we feel in a more concrete way, though getting it out on paper is only symbolic of our intention at this stage. It's part of the objectification—the separation—process. It's why I usually request a drawing from a client of what they see before a clearing and never after. Over a couple of weeks, perception becomes more acute and at the same time the cord becomes more defined. Using drawings to compare how we saw the cord at the beginning of our explorations to how we saw it at the end is interesting and instructive.

The observation process serves to separate the cord's effects from our own energy. Usually, it becomes more localised. It becomes obvious to us at this stage that it is a foreign energy—not like the feeling of "me." As it crystallizes out of our wider energy field to one local spot, we can detach from it more easily. But this still will not actually clear it. In most cases, especially with the toughest toxic cords, it's still necessary to get it done by a qualified clearer.

Chapter 37

Do I need a clearer or can I do it myself?

Most toxic cords need a trained, professional clearer.[29] In a few cases, the cords that form later in our lives might be light enough for us to see and detach from easily. If we can see these foreign influences as distinct from our own energy and discharge the emotion they contain, we might be able to let them go simply by intention. Often, however, these later cords lie on top of older, more stubborn cords that were laid down when we were very young.

In some cases of an old, badly entangled and noxious cord, a series of sessions with a qualified clearer followed by a clearing will be needed for an effective result. Such sessions are designed to help the client become more aware of his or her energy field. More than that, the process of focused exploration in deep states of awareness crystallizes the energy of a cord and separates it from the client's energy before a clearing. A properly conducted cord investigation with a clearer also has the invaluable benefit of teaching the client precisely what toxic cord energy feels like. Once we know, we can avoid relationships where a cord is likely to form and we can work on further differentiation that will mean we won't need cords to feel connected to those we love.

A qualified clearer has specific skills and perceptive abilities born of long experience. They've also engaged in an exacting training. Not everyone has the aptitude. Please be aware of, and avoid, well-intentioned but deluded people, calling themselves clearers or healers, who ask you to imagine a gigantic pair of scissors or something of the sort with which to cut the cord. Like wishful thinking, such purely mental efforts rarely work.

There's no harm in exploring what may be a toxic cord on your own in meditation or in reflection, if only to enable some detachment from the emotions carried in a cord. In the beginning, a cord is hard to differentiate from our own energy simply because it tends to be so mingled in it. If we're not aware of it as an emotional tug-of-war or open telephone line with another person, we might first feel it when it causes us sharp pain that appears not to have a physical cause. Or it might draw our attention to some unexpected but repeated sensation in our body that is noticeably associated with another person, such as a constriction in our chest when we think of our mother.

As a matter of course, sudden or persistent unexplained pain should always be checked by a qualified health practitioner whether a medical doctor, physiotherapist, chiropractor or osteopath. If there is no physical cause found and all tests are normal, that's when you might consider that it's an "energetic" pain caused by a samskara surfacing to our consciousness. Or, it might indicate a toxic cord.

When we become more aware of it, a cord feels foreign and intense in a tangible way that affects our emotions, our energy and/ or our physical comfort. Under observation, it can become very uncomfortable—but this discomfort is not permanent. It is simply a necessary part of the process of exploration that gives information on the dynamics of the cord. We then become hyperaware of the cord, and that increases sensitivity. When we are reasonably certain there is a toxic cord between us and another person, the next step is to "map" it through, putting our focused attention on it. This is when we might feel its shape, sense what it is made of, its texture and size. We need to know where it attaches on our body and the other person's. It might have a color. It might move in a certain way or be motionless.

It is important at this stage that we do not do anything to it. Trying to cut it mentally, pushing it back to the other person or ignoring it will only feed the cord with our resistance. In actual fact, simple conscious awareness does more to discharge most perverse energies than any frantic attempt to counter them.

The observation period of a cord takes some time, usually two to three weeks. Even if you do not have the advantage of a meditator's ability to focus attention within and to quiet the mind, simply becoming aware of your body and your energy in a quiet, relaxed mode can show you a great deal about the dynamics of the cord.

Nevertheless, it is tricky. If we have had a cord since the womb, with later ones piggybacked onto it, a foreign energy can often be misidentified as our own. Or we may not know who is at the other end, but just have an uneasy feeling of being dumped on or drained. We need to know exactly what it is and how it operates.

In some cases of not-too-toxic cords, simply becoming aware of it and how it operates can begin to dislodge it. Please remember that it is *not* by mental visualization that this occurs. Using creative visualization in this particular process often becomes a delusion based on wishful, magical thinking and is therefore ineffective as well as inaccurate.

Mapping a cord is best done in a relaxed, intuitive, receptive state. To be as accurate as possible, observe any emotional reactions or physical sensations you might have without worrying too much about what they might mean.

In cord-mapping sessions, I take the client into their Third Eye for deeper perception than just ordinary observation. This one-on-one technique for deep states of awareness connects the client to their Higher Self and an ability to bring consciousness into areas of the unconscious mind. You could equally think of it as increased access to the broader apperception and intuitive understanding of the right brain. In any case, in this state of deeper consciousness we can become aware of flows of energy, samskaras or wounds in the subtle bodies and parasitic energetic attachments such as cords and entities. Energy blocks can be shifted, old wounds can be resolved and old reactive patterns can be discharged in this very powerful technique. The advantage of having a trained practitioner to deepen the space, hold the energy, ask the right questions and bring you back from deep states as well as connect you to higher spiritual beings, is immense. It makes it all so much easier.

And for exceptionally sticky toxic cords, only a clearing in this professional setting by a trained clearer will do.

For a not-too-toxic cord, answering questions and exploring effects and beginnings can go far in mapping its astral structure. If it turns out to be more stubborn than at first appeared, the information you extract from observation can't hurt until you can find a clearer. However, there are some traps, and becoming aware of them means we can avoid them.

LEFT-BRAIN INTERFERENCE

One of the main functions of the left hemisphere of our brain is to analyze. It is verbal in expression and likes to chatter. It likes things to be neat, categorized and labeled. It prefers logical explanations. It doesn't like vagueness. It likes to be in control, with everything named and ordered and known. It notices details and sees differences that separate things and make them distinct. For most of us educated in Western traditions of thinking, the left brain is dominant.

The right hemisphere of the brain is creative and sees the big picture. It understands emotion, nonverbal communication, subtext and cues. It sees similarities and commonality. It's able to hold a number of possible viewpoints, belief systems or conflicting ideas without friction.

When I ask people questions in session about what they see or experience, sometimes—even in the deep inner space—their left brain automatically answers because it is used to being in charge. It wants to maintain control of the mind, to give the "right" response: the one that is logical or familiar, that makes sense or is plausible.

Three things usually happen when I ask a question in this context. The first thing that pops into their mind is usually the "right" answer, even when it makes no sense to them. It is what they are actually seeing, perceiving or experiencing. Almost immediately, however, the left brain tries to assert dominance by questioning this answer and negating it because it's not logical, and so there's a moment of confusion. The third step in this rapid process is when the left brain supplies what it thinks we ought to answer, what we ought to be seeing, but is merely what my teacher Samuel Sagan calls "astral video." People feeling the effects of this process usually apologize that they might just be making things up. Sometimes it is hard to tell the difference.

TELLING THE DIFFERENCE BETWEEN
WHAT IS THERE AND WHAT WE IMAGINE IS THERE

Let's try a mental exercise.

Imagine a mouse—a small white mouse. Make it Disney-cute. Give it perky ears, a pink nose and paws. Maybe it has a little red bow around its neck. Make it do something cute.

Notice how it feels to visualize this image. It's predictable and under your control.

Actually, after a while it might be a bit boring.

Now, let that image go. Close your eyes and quiet your mind. Take a little time for this.

Now, let the mouse that is already in your mind come into view there.

I'd like you to note the differences between this mouse and the first one, before you read what other people invariably see. How does it feel simply to observe this mouse? Can you make it do anything? Is it predictable? Boring?

Now you may read what others see, in the note on page 263.[30]

This exercise illustrates the difference between what has intrinsic meaning for us—the mouse that is there already in our consciousness, and the mouse we are actively, creatively imagining. It also shows how differently these two behave in our mind and how we feel when seeing them.

The artifact that we create visually has no life of its own. However, if our thinking mind, influenced by conditioned emotion—or someone else—were to make a suggestion, that artifact will assume those qualities or behaviors. In contrast, what we see that is already in our consciousness surprises us. It's unpredictable, often illogical. It's independent of our active imagination.

We can react to what we imagine and this gives it a pseudolife. This is how a child can imagine a witch under the bed or a monster behind the bedroom curtain, which then have power to frighten the child. Nevertheless, something about these bogeymen is predictable, even familiar. The shapes we imagine we see in a darkened alleyway or dark room are monsters we usually already know. At the back of our mind we know we're creating our own fear in this way. We can create other emotional reactions in ourselves in the same way by imagining a picture of something sad, or romantic or sexual. These are recognizable fantasies that do exactly as we direct. It's completely different if we simply observe what is there within us.

It means that if we can train ourselves to witness what arises to our consciousness without editorial by the chattering left brain, we have a chance of seeing what is of most importance and deepest meaning to us—even if it's neither logical nor making sense in the moment. If we simply accept what we have seen, without the need to explain it away, the experience can show us much about our inner landscape.

Even if you have no access to a practitioner of Inner Space Techniques, it is possible to train the left brain to do its usual great job of observing details without a chatty commentary. Through meditation we can simultaneously utilize the broad vision and holistic, intuitive understanding of the right brain to interpret what we are seeing. It's a true integration of left and right brain functions.

Chapter 38

Sacred space

We form cords with others from deep fears of being abandoned, rejected by those we love, being alone, unwanted, worthless. It's a fear at the core of our being. The attachments we make from this empty space are about connection and wanting to belong, perhaps with a subconscious memory of the infinite connectedness of the world of spirit from which we come. When we are desperate, we will connect even with someone cruel or manipulative, because any connection is better than feeling so alone and empty. To heal this deep void, we need a sacred space of *equal depth and power* to hold us in unconditional love, complete acceptance and safety.

In this sacred space a ritual lifts us out of the everyday and creates a connection with our Higher Self, or with the Divine energy, or with the creative power of the universe, or however you see it. It is a space in which our emptiness is filled with restorative light and our wounds are healed. A solemn ritual answers our capacity for profound meaning, a pause in our busy lives to acknowledge our need for spiritual nourishment and a commitment to a deeper life purpose or direction. It recognizes our need to be met in our deepest core by vast, eternal spiritual beings, to acknowledge our spiritual nature. A ritual gains power from the solemn repetition of many sincere practices, from the power of the Word spoken in truth, from the aspiration of the practitioner and participants to connect to the Divine light. In the space of a genuine ritual, all that is false and empty falls away and only the wholeness of the True Self is left.

For this reason, a cord clearing is a sacred ritual. It is a profound, life-changing event. Everyone experiences a clearing in a different way. Even in the case of having several clearings, each one will be unique. The following are some verbatim reports right after a clearing ritual: "I felt like the words took me to a different plane, where everything was going to be set right," "I felt very heavy, as though I was sinking into the floor. Then I felt something like a hand pulling the cord out of my middle." Another person said, "At first I knew the cord was sticking, not wanting to go, being difficult. Then all of a sudden something lifted, it all just went." For yet another participant it was, "As soon as you began the ritual it was ready to go. Then it just blew away, like a wind."

And in the weeks, months and years afterward? People report feeling lighter, different somehow, more present, more themselves. Clearing cords gives us back our energy, our space and our lives to share as we wish.

Endnotes

1   A Rescuer is only one of myriad Characters people can mistakenly believe
    they are. Characters are conditioned subpersonalities, false selves we have
    developed to survive intense childhood experiences. They have a programed
    mind set and predictable behaviors. We can identify with them and often,
    when our Character takes over, we find we're behaving in a way we'd prefer
    not to. For a complete examination of Characters and how we can become
    free of them, see Carruthers, A., (2008) *Let Your Past Go and Live.* Allen &
    Unwin, Sydney Australia.

2   In 1969, psychiatrist John Bowlby was the first in his field to theorize that the
    early relationship with a parent has lasting effect throughout life. He called it
    Attachment Theory.

3   In the 1960s and '70s psychologist Mary Ainsworth further researched Bowl-
    by's attachment theories and developed an experiment for toddlers called
    Strange Situation. She categorized three main styles of early childhood attach-
    ment: *secure attachment, anxious-ambivalent attachment* and *anxious-avoidant
    attachment.* In 1990, Ainsworth's colleague Mary Main added a fourth cate-
    gory which Ainsworth agreed was valid: *disorganized/disoriented attachment.*
    See Ainsworth, M. and Bowlby, J., (1965) *Child Care and the Growth of Love.*
    Penguin Books, London; Ainsworth, M., (1967) *Infancy in Uganda.* Johns
    Hopkins, Baltimore; Ainsworth, M. Blehar, M. Waters, E. and Wall, S., (1978)
    Patterns of Attachment. Erlbaum, Hillsdale, NJ.

4   Couvade syndrome occurs when the father experiences pregnancy symptoms
    and/or labor pain. See Bainbridge, D., (2000) *Making Babies: The science of
    pregnancy.* Harvard University Press, Cambridge MA; Merskey, H., "Pain and
    Psychological Medicine" in P.D. Wall & R. Melzack (eds), (1994) *The Text-
    book of Pain.* Churchill Livingstone, Edinburgh; BBC News, "Men Suffer

from Phantom Pregnancy," June 14, 2007, online at <http://news.bbc.co .uk/2/hi/6751709.stm?lsm>, accessed November 30, 2010.

5 In the Clairvision School of Meditation, for example, the Column of Spirit is cultivated in practices as part of "subtle body building" to develop lasting connections to spiritual realms.

6 "Ego" in this context, when I give it a capital letter, is not the small, grasping, self-centered ego. Nor is it the ego of Freud or Jung. It is a Higher Ego or in-carnating spirit. Similarly, "Archetype" in this context refers to the blueprint of our individuality, a higher design that guides our evolution in this life.

7 Winnicott, D.W., (1964) *The Child, the Family, and the Outside World.* Pelican, London; Winnicott, D.W., (1949) "Mind and its Relation to the Psyche-Soma," in *Through Pediatrics to Psycho-Analysis*, Hogarth Press and The Institute of Psycho-Analysis, London, pp. 243–54.

8 Cooper, G., Hoffman, K., Marvin, R. and Powell, B., (2000) Circle of Security Project, online at <http://www.circleofsecurity.org/treatmentassumptions .html>, accessed May 7, 2010. This direct quote and the concepts in the fol-lowing paragraphs derive from the research and therapeutic interventions of these authors.

9 Cooper, et al, Circle of Security Project.

10 Main, M. and Hesse, E., "Parents' unresolved traumatic experiences are re-lated to infant disorganized attachment status," in Greenberg, M.T., Cicchetti, D. and Cummings, E.M. (eds) (1990) *Attachment in the Preschool Years*, Uni-versity of Chicago Press, Chicago.

11 Main and Hesse, "Parents' unresolved traumatic experiences."

12 Winnicott, D.W., (1971) *Playing and Reality*, Routledge, London.

13 Butler, D., and Moseley, L., (2008) *Explain Pain.* Noigroup Publications, Ad-elaide, p. 24.

14 McTaggart, L., (2007) *The Intention Experiment.* Free Press, New York. Much of this book details historical and modern experimentation, and scientific demonstrations of the energy exchange between all matter—animate and in-animate.

15 A Suicidal Character is differentiated from a true death wish, as the Charac-ter is really acting out a wish to punish others, or it is a cry for help that the person cannot otherwise express. While the thoughts of a Suicidal Character are bleak and hopeless, there is a tinge of melodrama to the mind-set.

16 Winnicott, *Playing and Reality.*

17 Sheldrake, R., (1999) *Dogs that know when their owners are coming home.* Three Rivers Press, Random House, London.

18 Masterson, J., (1995) *The Real Self.* Brunner/Mazel, Inc., New York.

19 These include: Narcissistic Personality Disorder, Borderline Personality Disorder, Histrionic Personality Disorder and others. American Psychiatric Association, (2000) *Diagnostic and Statistical Manual of Mental Disorders*, 4th ed. American Psychiatric Association, Washington, DC.

20 Masterson, J., (1993) *The Emerging Self: A developmental, self, and object relations approach to the treatment of the closet narcissistic disorder of the self.* Brunner/Mazel, Inc., New York.

21 Yudofsky, S., (2005) *Fatal Flaws: Navigating destructive relationships with people with disorders of personality and character.* American Psychiatric Publishing, Washington, DC, pp. 15, 16.

22 In Professor Yudofsky's estimation, in some people personality flaws are dangerous, but they might also have qualities that may be seen as assets. "When people are unwilling to acknowledge their personality or character problems or are unable to change their damaging behaviors, they are disabled by what I term *fatal* flaws." *Fatal Flaws,* p. xi.

23 Butler, et al, *Explain Pain*, p. 21.

24 Schnarch, D., (1997) *Passionate Marriage.* Henry Holt and Company Inc, New York.

25 Zdenek, M., (1985) *The Right Brain Experience: An intimate program to free the powers of your imagination.* McGraw-Hill Book Company, New York.

26 Bad seating posture, for example slouching for long periods of sitting in meditation, can cause compression of the jugular veins and spinal vertebrae. This can reduce the supply of cerebrospinal fluid, which carries neurotransmitters to the brain and flushes metabolic waste. It can result in an inability to concentrate, short attention span, forgetfulness and headaches.

27 Ghose, A., Next Step in Evolution, Development of Supramental, online at <http://www.cosmicharmony.com/Sp/Aurobndo/Aurobndo.htm#Supramental>, accessed November 11, 2010.

28 Lutz, A., Greischar, L., Rawlings, N., Ricard, M., and Davidson, R., (2004) "Long-term meditators self-induce high-amplitude gamma synchrony during mental practice," *Proceedings of the National Academy of Sciences of the United States of America,* online at http://www.pnas.org/content/101/46/16369.full.pdf+html, accessed October 18, 2009.

29 The author can be contacted at <www.avrilcarruthers.com> and is based in Sydney, Australia. An international list of other professional clearers is available at <www.clairvision.org>.

30 Invariably people tell me that the *mouse that is already there* in their mind is brown, gray or black, that it moves without being made to do so and that it has its own look and its own quirks and is not especially cute. In fact, it's often a wild mouse.

Index

Index

Index

If you enjoyed this book, visit

www.tarcherbooks.com

and sign up for Tarcher's e-newsletter to receive
special offers, giveaway promotions, and
information on hot upcoming releases.

TARCHER
PENGUIN

Great Lives Begin with Great Ideas

Connect with the Tarcher Community

· · ·

Stay in touch with favorite authors!
Enter weekly contests!
Read exclusive excerpts!
Voice your opinions!

Follow us

 Tarcher Books

 @TarcherBooks

If you would like to place a bulk order
of this book, call 1-800-847-5515.